Prepublication Comments

"A therapist, trainer, and longtime meditator, Lind-Kyle (When Sleeping Beauty Wakes Up) writes superbly about the relationship between meditation and the brain. Dividing her book into two sections, she begins with an in-depth scientific discussion of the anatomy of the brain, its evolution, and how our thought processes work. Using an electroencephalograph, Lind-Kyle has been able to measure and monitor mind states and identify when brain waves are out of balance. She presents brain research that shows how meditation can reshape the nature of the mind. In Part 2, readers will find detailed discussion of how using mind-training techniques can help them access the centers of the brain in order to bring about change in their mindset and thought patterns."

—Phyllis Goodman, *Library Journal*

"Heal Your Mind, Rewire Your Brain is fascinating, practical, and absolutely essential for everyone, but especially aging baby boomers. Everyone should know what's in this book."

—Christiane Northrup, MD, Author of *The Secret Pleasures of Menopause* and *Women's Bodies, Women's Wisdom*

"A brilliant journey through the brain-mind, by a courageous traveler who knows the territory firsthand. A must read for any serious explorer of Consciousness."

—Alberto Villoldo, PhD, Author of *Shaman, Healer, Sage*

"Heal Your Mind, Rewire Your Brain is a rich, beautifully conceived book, which combines science and meditation in a thought provoking and understandable fashion! Patt Lind-Kyle explains why meditation works and how to use it effectively. For all of us who need answers to the whys of meditation, this is THE book to read. For those of you who are skeptical about the benefits of meditation, this book will put an end to your skepticism. It is exquisitely written and opens new doors to one's soul...a remarkable piece!"

—Elisa Bongiovanni, JD and Corporate Counsel

"Heal Your Mind, Rewire Your Brain: Applying the Exciting New Science of Brain Synchrony for Creativity, Peace, and Presence *was a pleasure to read. Having spent the last forty years researching the brain's connection to mind, and elucidating the important role of brain wave phase synchrony to consciousness, I was pleased to read how our new knowledge can change one's life in many ways. Mental training exercises lead to a new way of being in the world. The author writes in an easy-to-read, entertaining style. If you have interest in meditation of any kind, this is the book for you."*

—Les Fehmi, PhD, Author of *The Open-Focus Brain: Harnessing the Power of Attention to Heal Mind and Body*

"Neuroscience's insights into the plasticity of the brain are often heady—and often equally confusing—for the lay reader. And even if people are familiar with the research, they usually do not know how to apply the findings in their daily lives. This book digests the past ten years of brain-mind research and helps people make transformative breakthroughs. With specific exercises and practices, brain-mind meditations, and nutritional information, Patt Lind-Kyle shows us how to access our inner world to reduce stress, balance emotions, open creativity, and reunite the psyche with the soul. Well-written and groundbreaking."

—Don Richard Riso and Russ Hudson, best-selling authors of *The Wisdom of the Enneagram* and *Personality Types*

"Discoveries in cutting-edge brain research—known as neuroplasticity—have opened doors to our greatest potential for healing, learning, refining, and expanding most of the body-mind functions directed by our brains. This new book, Patt Lind-Kyle's second, explains this science in down-to-earth terms, and describes simple exercises by which we can each reap its amazing benefits in our own lives. Whether your goal is to find greater peace of mind, to refine a present skill, or to master a brand new body of knowledge, you'll find this book invaluable. The author's discussions of the implications of this new science, as well as its applications in our lives, are as practical as they are informative. A must-read for anyone interested in creating a better life."

—Hal Zina Bennett, PhD, Author of *The Lens of Perception: A User's Guide to Higher Consciousness*

"What a delightful read! Patt Lind-Kyle beautifully weaves together in a very understandable way not only the latest knowledge in brain research but combines this with her intensive experience in meditation and deep commitment to giving the reader practical exercises that make a difference. Heal Your Mind, Rewire Your Brain allows you to experience peace, stillness, and a renewed creativity and delight with your life."

—Linda Fitch, Executive Director, The Four Winds Society, and Dean of the Healing the Light Body School

"In Heal Your Mind, Rewire Your Brain, Patt Lind-Kyle shares a treasure trove of wisdom and practical guidance that will allow anyone to quiet their mind, reconnect with their inner guidance, and make the kinds of choices and decisions that will allow them to lead healthier, happier, and more meaningful personal and professional lives. We are delighted to use Patt's book as an integral part of our consulting and coaching practice."

—Joyce Dowdall, Managing Partner, Generative Leadership Group

"In her inimitable style, Patt Lind-Kyle addresses brain-wave pattern synchrony, and its harmonization, with insight and courage. Moving with directness and kindness toward those new to the ideas, she embraces readers with ease and imagination. She has the knack of making ideas come alive, and she conquers large concepts step-by-step...all with manageable language and logic. And her story makes sense instantly. Focused on meditation as mind training, Patt's experiences ring true; her authenticity is palpable. Heal Your Mind, Rewire Your Brain is a first-rate approach to the whys, wherefores, and hows that can contribute to manifesting creativity, peace, and presence in the world."

—A. Harris Stone, EdD, Founder and Chancellor, the Graduate Institute of Connecticut

"Patt Lind-Kyle has accomplished a remarkable feat, bringing together fascinating neuroscience and effective self-development tools in the same book. Add to that her warmth, wisdom, and clinical skill and you have a refreshing joy of a read to boot! Bravo."

—Emmett Miller, MD, Author of *Deep Healing* and *Our Culture on the Couch*

"Heal Your Mind, Rewire Your Brain *is a powerful owner's manual for your brain and mind, complete with a "Mental Tool Chest" to help free you from the stress and suffering of habitual negative emotional patterning. These mental training practices provide nothing short of a scientific and practical road map to peace, happiness, and mind-body freedom.*

Author Patt Lind-Kyle leads us by the hand on a fascinating tour of the brain's architecture and physiology. She inspires us and shows us what is possible through the regular practice of mental training and meditation. Her empowering message is that we actually do have the ability to rewire our brains for greater health and well-being."

—Brian J. Breiling, PsyD, Psychotherapist, Coach, and Author/ Editor of *Light Years Ahead: The Illustrated Guide to Full Spectrum and Colored Light in Mindbody Healing*

"Although the brain has always had remarkable ability to heal itself and to adapt to new situations, the science of neuroplasticity has finally emerged to prove the ultimate human potential. Thinking sets in motion spiritual forces to bring about change. Heal Your Mind, Rewire Your Brain *provides radical tools to assist you in your own personal evolution toward peace and health."*

—C. Norman Shealy, MD, PhD, President Emeritus, Holos University Graduate Seminary

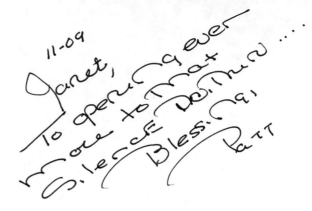

11-09
Janet,
To opening ever
more to that
silence within ....
Blessings,
Patt

Heal Your Mind,
Rewire Your Brain

Applying the Exciting New Science
of Brain Synchrony for Creativity,
Peace, and Presence

Patt Lind-Kyle

Energy Psychology Press
Santa Rosa, CA 95403
www.EnergyPsychologyPress.com

Cataloging-in-Publication Data

Lind-Kyle, Patt.
Heal your mind, rewire your brain : applying the exciting new science of brain synchrony for creativity, peace, and presence / Patt Lind-Kyle.
     p. cm.
Includes bibliographical references and index.
ISBN: 978-1-60415-056-8
1. Mental healing. 2. Neuroplasticity. 3. Brain. I. Title.
RZ400.L56 2009

615.8'51—dc22

2009030120

Typeset in Warnock Pro and Mona Lisa Solid
Printed in USA
Typeset by Karin Kinsey
Edited by Stephanie Marohn
Author photograph by Dee Le Van
Cover Design by Victoria Valentine
10 9 8 7 6 5 4 3 2 1

To David
Who is such a gift

Contents

Acknowledgments

I have deep appreciation and gratitude for all the people who supported and guided me in the incredible journey of creating this book. I could not have done something this challenging by myself.

In the beginning of my meditation experience, I found my first real meditation teacher, Rina Sircar, whom I treasure. I am grateful to all the other teachers who encouraged me to follow the meditative path. I am also grateful to all my students and clients who were willing to have me view their brain waves and who continue to teach me so much about the brain. A special thank you to Joyce Dowdall for encouraging me to write this book. I'm indebted to the scientists who have dedicated their lives to their research and their curiosity about the brain. I honor deeply the Dalai Lama for his inspiration and encouragement to researchers to study how meditation changes the brain.

Once the book was born, John Nelson did a remarkable job of clarifying its message. I so appreciated the direction and encouragement from my friend Hal Bennett. Dawson Church, publisher of Energy Psychology Press, saw the potential in the book. I was overjoyed with his foresight and believing in the importance and timeliness of the book. Thank you, Midpoint staff, for your practical feedback on presenting the book in the best possible way. My editor, Stephanie Marohn, helped me shape the book into its present form and did a remarkable job of finding things I had missed.

Last, but most important, I want to give my thanks to my partner, David, with whom I am so blessed to be. Words cannot express his love, support, and unending encouragement of me.

Thank you all.

Preface

I have often asked myself, "Why do some people have a keen interest in becoming more aware and finding meaning in their lives and in their own forward evolution, while others remain unconscious to its possibility for them?" In search of my own answer, I have focused my attention for the past thirty-seven years on two avenues of inquiry. The first is how to make sense of my daily life with its personal and interpersonal challenges. The second, and in many ways the more important, is trying to understand what role the mind plays in my being happy and peaceful. This search for understanding has been a yearning, a strong pull, and a discontent throughout my life, and I am excited to share some of what I've discovered.

In these critical times of stress, financial struggles, and mental chaos, it seems imperative that genuine compassion for ourselves and others becomes the focal point for an evolutionary shift in our society. As we rub shoulders with our friends, neighbors, and coworkers, we can feel in many people a deep pain and unhappiness. If we walk down the street of any major city, we can see the evolutionary impact of an increasingly complex and technological culture. If we stand back and watch people hurrying past us, we realize that many, despite their modern attire, are no different from our distant ancestors. Like our ancestors, they compete for their survival by besting or being bested by the circumstances and people around them. On the street, we can also see men and woman that are sensitive to the relationship between themselves and others; they reach out to talk and laugh and touch each other affectionately. Some sit in the shadows in a drug-induced fantasy trying to block out the world around them. Others are trying to "make it big"; they hurry down the street, dressed in thousand-dollar suits, tapping out messages on their Blackberries or talking on cell phones glued to their ears.

We all recognize these types among our friends and acquaintances. Even more interesting, however, is to recognize what each type represents. The modern cavemen, the connectors, the visionaries, and the strivers each reflect in metaphoric terms the natural evolutionary development of our brain. Our magnificent brain has evolved to teach us how to survive, how to relate, how to dream, and how to find success in our life. To survive in the early period of human existence, we evolved the old brain of fight or flight; to experience feelings and family connections, we evolved the emotional or mammalian part of the brain; to create and imagine new worlds, we evolved the neocortex or new brain; and finally we evolved the prefrontal lobes that integrate these functions and offer the possibility of compassion and success, and the creation of a positive future for ourselves.

These behaviors and brain functions are mostly played out unconsciously in us from infancy to childhood to midlife and into old age. Some of us, however, wake up and discover that we are mindlessly going through life with no meaning and become unsure of why we are doing what we are doing. When we become aware of the habitual and automatic attitudes, thoughts, and behaviors that are determining our life conditions, we make another step in our personal evolution. Evolution requires change. We all hesitate to make changes. This natural hesitation is the result of knowing that change involves taking risks, and that is scary. Change moves us out of our comfort zone. When faced with this fear of change, we need to ask ourselves the question: "Is the pain and fear I am experiencing greater than the change itself?" To have the courage to take the step into awareness sets us on an amazing evolutionary journey of discovery.

Like everyone else faced with change, I experienced pain and fear and had many questions when I took the step into my own personal unknown. Two processes helped me: meditation and a drive to understand my mind and brain. Meditation first unraveled my deepest questions and gave me answers not found in traditional study. Through meditation, I became fascinated with how my brain related to the mind states I was experiencing in meditation. What I have since discovered in the years of deep meditation and brain-mind research is that each structure of the brain is characterized by a specific brain wave, and that focusing on each one separately brings a synchronization of these brain waves. I found that it is also possible to clear dysfunctional attitudes and behaviors and to open to a state of whole brain-mind integration, which created in me a state of happiness and loving kindness.

Over the years, I have come to call meditation a form of mind training. Our minds can be trapped by their own mental states and can put us into frantic and depressed conditions. Mind training helps focus our attention, quiets a scattered mind, and brings the flexibility and clarity that enable us to see other options. The purpose of this book is to share what I've learned about the nature of the mind, how it interfaces with brain structures, and how meditation or mind training can help you find happiness and peace of mind. If you have not meditated before, you will be surprised at how easily meditation can calm your mind and open your heart.

I have explored the inner workings of the mind and brain in many different ways. In 1970, I was a college professor, recently divorced and looking for something to fill my heart. At that time, it did not seem to be men or parties. I was watching TV one day and a program popped up on the screen in which a woman was describing meditation. I was not familiar with meditation. As I watched, she had the audience close their eyes and follow their breath. I followed her instructions. I had never done this before, but I was amazed at my response. In just a short time, I felt relaxed and my mind finally became quiet. This felt good. A few months later, this woman gave a presentation in town. At the end of the session, she invited people to join a group and meditate weekly together. I meditated with one of these groups for several years.

Four years after I began mediating, I heard about a new graduate school where meditation was part of the curriculum. Within months, I applied to this school to get another graduate degree, this one in East/West psychology. My time there is one of the highlights in my life. At the school, I met faculty member Rina Sircar, a Buddhist nun from Burma who teaches meditation. I feel very blessed to have had the opportunity to attend many mediation retreats lead by Rena.

Soon after graduate school, I resigned my teaching position and started a new learning center. Within a few years, however, chronic fatigue and immune dysfunction syndrome (CFIDS) hit me quite suddenly. But this experience created an opportunity for a healing process that was truly miraculous. Most doctors were not familiar with my illness at the time and could not help me. I discovered how to heal myself from this debilitating condition. Looking back, I realize that I fell naturally into a healing approach that followed the way the brain works. After continually studying the new brain research, I've come to understand how that healing happened. One of the most important aspects of my healing was the use of meditation to remove my negative thoughts about myself and help bring my body back into a natural balance.

Five years after my healing, I had an experience on a dark, stormy night in Portland, Oregon, that changed everything. I stopped at the gates of our home and got out to open them. As I began to walk toward the gate, my old Jeep started to roll forward. I jumped up on the running board, but as the Jeep veered off the road and over the embankment, I was thrown, fell hard on my bottom, and broke my tailbone. Within three days, an enormous amount of energy was shooting through my body. It came in the form of a roar, heat, and excited intensity. I felt as if I had been turned inside out and was being rewired. A friend described this electric experience as Kundalini energy surging up my spine. This is a yogic view of how the body, brain, and mind are rewired to experience a different state of consciousness. This experience was a major turning point in my life.

As the months passed, my tailbone healed and my energy began to rebalance itself. After the completion of that experience, I was a different person. A major shift had taken place and I struggled to integrate what was happening to me. In the process, I became fascinated with the mind, spending hours every day meditating at home as well as attending many weeklong retreats. I never seemed to get enough of the meditation. Fundamentally, after weeklong retreats, I felt that I never quite "got it." I just wasn't getting what I sensed this yearning was pulling me toward, even in longer ten-day retreats. I came to the conclusion that I needed to spend a much longer time in retreat. With the good graces of my sweet, understanding family, I attended my first three-month retreat.

In this long retreat, the formal meditation sittings and walking practice began at 4:00 a.m. and continued until 9:00 p.m. At first, this meditation practice seemed impossible both because of the intensity of the meditation and the schedule. Once I got used to the daily rhythm, however, and with the silent support of one hundred retreat participants and periodic meetings with a teacher, the concentrated mental energy began to work its magical transformation. After three months, the day finally came to "break silence." When we finally spoke, one of the participants said, "It feels like we are all patients in ICU recovering from open-heart surgery." It certainly was a heart opening experience for most of us. And it was an amazing inner process of personal development for me. When I returned home, family members commented, "Where did your anger go?" My anger had noticeably reduced and been replaced with love for myself, which I had never felt.

That first three-month long meditation experience was so life-changing that it encouraged me to attend another three-month retreat the following year. These long retreats continued and culminated with a six-month silent retreat. I ended up in a little trailer on the grounds of a meditation retreat facility. I cooked my own food and set my own schedule. This setup allowed me to let go of any patterns and just let myself be. I began to live in a peace that, as the Bible says, "surpasses all understanding." This peace released me from prior stress and I lost the strain of striving. I also felt released from the need for purpose. I settled into a simple acceptance and had the awareness that in every person—beneath their tension, anxiety, and pressure—lies this incredible source of peace and happiness.

Through these retreats, I followed the yearning of my discontent to discover the answer to my lifelong question of how to find peace in my life. But I still had questions about how internal mental states work. I wanted to know what specifically interrupts and invades our naturally peaceful mind, and shifts us back into the state of being tense, resistant, and discontented. I also had the question of what allows the mind to periodically and naturally fall back into a state of peace.

Two years later some of my questions were answered. Serendipity introduced me to a neurofeedback monitoring technique, an electroencephalograph system called the Brain Mirror. It provides a way to measure and monitor mind states. It can be used, for instance, to understand what is happening during meditation. I was excited to have found a tool that could help me understand these brain-mind states, identify when the brain waves are out of balance, and show me when and how my mind became busy, fearful, or stressed.

I bought one of these systems and began using it to explore what the brain did when in different mental states. I began to understand how brain-wave patterns integrated the mind with the brain functions. At the same time, I began to study neuroscience: the scientific study of the molecular, cellular, physiological, and psychological processes of the brain and nervous system. Through these scientific pursuits, I gained a context for how our mind, brain, and nervous system fit together. From my experience with meditation and consciousness, I realized that with the right instruction people could discover how to control their mental states and clear the dysfunctional patterning in their brain structures. I became impassioned about how consciously working with the brain and the mind can be used to heal, as well as bring the brain back into an amazing balance of creativity and presence. This book results from my passion to share this vital information.

Introduction

Years ago, I was facilitating a hospice grief group for people who had recently lost a loved one. As we sat in a circle, each person shared his or her story of grief. Suddenly, one man in the circle burst into deep, sobbing cries. Just like a baby, his tears resounded from his toes. He had been married for sixty years, and his wife had just died of cancer. His cries echoed in my body for days and weeks. His suffering triggered a thought that kept coming back to me. I kept saying to myself, "He has no refuge. He has no place to go other than the physical memory of being with his wife. And now his grief comes from not being with her." The man's sadness was a reminder of how many people are trapped in their pain.

Studying the natural unfolding processes of the brain-mind has shown me how we can find a refuge from our pain, a home within. As you will discover as we move through this book, I am passionate about understanding how the brain works, how our mind functions, and how the two together enable us to take a huge leap in our evolution. That leap brings us to what I call our inner "home base" and allows us to reach our full potential in life.

As I noted in the preface, with every leap in human evolution, the human brain developed an additional brain center. Every evolutionary shift has changed the way we perceive who we are and how we experience the world in which we live. Almost every aspect of human experience, including love, memory, dreams, as well as our predisposition to religious thought, can be traced to one of these brain centers and the mental states they induce.

Heal Your Mind, Rewire Your Brain: Applying the Exciting New Science of Brain Synchrony for Creativity, Peace, and Presence is about the beauty and adaptability of the human brain and its innate ability to constantly change and adapt to external conditions, which is how we survive and thrive on this planet. The brain's ability to remold itself opens up enormous possibilities for us to make conscious changes and improvements in our life today. As we learn to train our minds and change our brains, we will ultimately evolve a more refined and satisfying quality of life for ourselves.

In fact, the brain's inherent transformational process can serve as a model or guide for how we can train our mind to be less intense and busy, and free from chaos, fear, pain, and inner wounds. We can train our mind to move into a silent, peaceful landscape of unbelievable possibilities. We can consciously train the mind to shift its movement from busy to quiet, from reactionary to calm and accepting, and from sensations into bodily awareness.

Heal Your Mind, Rewire Your Brain provides an overview of scientific perspectives on the brain-mind and shows how personally evolving your own brain can help change your life in any direction you desire. Evolving and changing your brain-mind requires engaging in some mental training practices. These can be transforming as they integrate your brain-mind and change your response to yourself and to life. From these practices, it is possible for you to discover a new way of being in the world and an increased sense of emotional balance and physical health. The two parts of this book will provide you with insights and understanding about how your own brain-mind interface and give you practical mental tools to use your brain-mind in ways beneficial for your well-being.

Part I of this book describes the history of how the brain evolved into its current design, how that affects every aspect of daily life, and how the brain-mind can be trained to interface more optimally with the environment and to develop diverse new capabilities.

The human brain has evolved over 650 million years to arrive at its current stage of development. Only recently in this time scale did it develop objective consciousness, or the ability to look back and examine itself. Today it is said that the brain is the last frontier of physiological research. Scientists continually design new research tools for uncovering the brain's mysteries. They tell us that the brain is the most complex networking system in the known universe. It has many parts that systematically interact, connect, and function in a remarkable arrangement of electrical pulses and chemical reactions. It is astonishing to consider that the brain is just a three-pound tofu-like structure that sits on the top of our spinal cord. Its job is to regulate our physical functioning and emotional behaviors. As noted, it has taken a good bit of time to arrive at this complex structure.

The brain has periodically taken dramatic leaps in size and functionality to increase human consciousness. The last "leap" was around one hundred thousand years ago, when the brain doubled in size in a short period of time. In our "newly" evolved brain, it is possible to become consciously focused and fully engaged in whatever we are doing, to ride the energies of all the brain centers and become highly creative. There is also an inner and outer brain-mind interaction that keeps us energized and enlivened. This is a state of consciousness that follows an energy pattern that circulates throughout the brain and body. This is the notion of "flow," which moves in the direction of the prefrontal lobes, the area of self-awareness that gathers meaning from the external world. Carl Jung has called this flow between the inner and outer experience of reality "synchronicity," or beyond the physical world's experience. By whatever name, this flow has been the focus of many spiritual traditions and is best represented by a sense of being alive or joyful.

Most of us find, however, that our experience of flow can get easily disrupted. Scientists say that this fluid integrated state is difficult to maintain because of a fundamental flaw: The brain has not been redesigned after the addition of new brain centers at each stage of its evolutionary development, leaving us with a somewhat inelegant design. The result is that there are communication flaws that affect the natural energy flow circulating within the brain. These imperfections become quite pronounced with the communication connections between our internal awareness and the way we interact with the outer world. These flaws can cut off the natural flow of energy from our outer experience and create an imbalance in our brain-mind system.

Due to these design flaws, we are limited in our ability to flick off the mental switch when life is counterproductive for us. How many of us have been in a situation in which we have been attacked either physically or verbally? We generally fight back to protect ourselves and stay in the conflict, ignoring our inner knowledge that tells us to stop escalating or get out of the destructive situation. In fact, rather than hearing this inner voice, we usually press harder to match the force of the situation. We pay less attention to our inner resources than to the outside world. We find it difficult to flip off the switch when an action is having the opposite result of what we desire.

We can take the idea of not listening to this inner direction a step further and look at how we become so driven and stressed-out in our daily lives. We all seem to be caught up in our fast-paced society with little time for our loved ones or ourselves. We are constantly on the go, with a cell phone in one hand and a PDA in the other. In fact, many of us drive, walk, and sleep with these devices. When we are in so-called relaxation, we are filling our time with movies, television, and computers. We are always connected with the outside world but find little time to reflect, be quiet, and find connection to our inner selves. This switch to our inner world is off, and we don't know how to turn it on. The Buddha called this condition suffering. Today we call it stress, which is being out of balance with no time to rest and reset the very system that will bring us back to a natural flow. In this book, we look at how the nervous system's flight-or-fight mechanism works and when to turn off this switch.

The brain-mind gives us support as we become aware of the need to make a change and flip the switch. Herein lies the magnificence of the brain's fine wiring system. *Heal Your Mind, Rewire Your*

Brain explains that the neuronal pathways (the brain's wiring system) can be altered and changes made to how we feel, think, and behave and how the body responds to stressful situations. Yes, it takes effort and some training, but these flaws can be rewired in the light of conscious awareness and disciplined practice.

Each new addition of the brain evolved because of the interaction of early humans with their ever-changing environment. It is the neural networking that connects all three layers or centers of the brain (reptilian, limbic, and cortex) together and is the means for the brain-mind to continue to evolve even today. As you learn new skills, try out new activities, expand your thinking, and deepen your feeling, you are evolving and changing your neuronal pathways. You are constantly rewiring your brain and changing the nature of your life.

The mental training tools presented in part II provide a conscious means of rewiring the neural network and affecting the functioning of the brain. The evolutionary design route of the three brain structures guides us into a natural way of training our minds in meditation to bring us mental and physical balance, and a stable quality of mind and physical well-being.

As you become more skillful in using the mental tools, the various mind states connect to and align the brain patterns in the neocortex (the newest part of the brain, in the cerebral cortex), the limbic center (the emotional brain), and the reptilian brain (the old or ancient brain). The sense of inner flow this interaction creates between brain centers turns off the "flaw switch." In training the mind, we reverse the evolutionary route the brain took in its development, and train in the opposite direction from the complex to the simple rudimentary brain centers. When the order is reversed, the mind tools link to each brain structure and create mental connection and synergy much like the Russian nesting dolls that are contained inside each other.

Remember the adage "You can't teach an old dog new tricks"? Well, it just isn't true. We are not stuck with our "old" brains because, as you'll discover in this book, our brains exhibit a high degree of adaptability to change. Scientists call this neuroplasticity, or how the brain can change the size of its structures and also their functions by strengthening the neuronal connections between different areas of the brain.

Tiger Woods, the world's premier golfer, is an example of how practice can restructure the brain and generate a high degree of skill through neuroplasticity. At age fourteen, Tiger started working with a psychologist who gave him techniques for relaxation, visualization, and focus to enhance his golf skills. He practiced different kinds of mental drills to improve his concentration. His father would also create distractions to teach his son focused attention. When Tiger was in the middle of a backswing, his father would cough or jiggle coins in his pocket. Such practices helped Tiger train his mind to stay focused, flexible, and calm under pressure. This has been the greatest key to his success. For all his physical abilities, it has been said that Tiger's greatest advantage is his "golf" brain.

Research has shown that meditation practice can actually increase the size of specific brain areas. We can mentally change our brain structure, increase brain cells, and modify neuronal pathways through our life experiences. Meditation and mind-training work is at the heart of making positive changes in every area of life. At the most basic level, this type of training improves mental stability and bestows a healthier immune system. A stable, focused, and calm mind reduces stress, which results in less illness and emotional fatigue.

By training the mind through meditation and other mental practices, it is possible to alter the brain's neuronal connections and circuitry that are responsible for emotions, behaviors, and perceptions, and thereby reshape the brain structure and change the way the brain functions. As we alter the brain circuitry, we are changing our mind, both figuratively and literally.

In part II of this book, you will learn meditation practices and mind tools to deal with the challenges and potentials of each brain center. The practices appear in four chapters, each of which explores a brain-wave pattern (beta, alpha, theta, delta), its associated key neurotransmitter chemical (dopamine, acetylcholine, GABA, serotonin), and the brain center in which it occurs. Research on brain waves has discovered that the messages from your mind tell your brain what to do, which then sends messages throughout your brain and body. These messages enable us to learn to play the piano, ride a bicycle, or type on a computer, among other complex activities. Research now shows that electrical brain-wave pulses have to have a chemical partner such as a neurotransmitter to send these messages via the nervous system. The mind is the energy that forms the patterns that ride the flow of these chemical and electrical interactions.

From the exercises and practices in part II, you can construct a daily training program to develop your mental capacities and flexibility. The more you practice these processes, the more skillful you will become and the more effective at rewiring your brain in your daily life. The guided meditations for each of the four brain-wave patterns will increase your ability to change both your brain and your mind. Remember, the neuroplasticity and adaptability of the brain is the leading edge of your own personal evolution. The more you change your mind, the more you change your brain. The more your brain changes, the more your mind evolves. In this way, you will heal your mind and discover your home base within, a source of peace, calm, and vitality in your life.

PART I

THE BRAIN'S STORY

1

The Mind and the Brain

The mind can only do what it is equipped to do. And so man must find out what kind of brain he has before he can understand his own behavior.

—Gay Gaer Luce and Julius Segal

While attending a long silent meditation retreat, I had the sudden and startling experience of losing my mind. The experience occurred near the end of the retreat. After months of the retreat, I had long settled into the daily meditation routine. I would wake up at 4:00 a.m., roll out of bed onto my meditation pillow, and sit for hours. On this fateful day, I got up early as usual and immediately began to meditate. My attention and concentration were strong and I went quickly and deeply into a lucid state of awareness. At the end of the sitting session, I took a break to use the rest room. As I washed my hands, I became aware of the mirror above the washbasin. But when I raised my head and looked into the mirror, I couldn't see myself. I was shocked. I turned away, looked back again at the mirror, but still didn't perceive my reflection. It was not there. I felt my face with my hands and confirmed that I could feel my nose, lips, and so on, but the reflection of my face was not in the mirror.

Still in shock, I tried to rationalize what was happening. I wondered if something had happened physically to the rods and cones in my eyes. Or metaphysically, was I in that nonmaterial mind that didn't reflect my self-perceived identity in the mirror? Many more questions came, and as they did, my image slowly reemerged in the mirror.

All of us have moments in our lives that, in looking back, become major turning points in our search for meaning, reality, or truth—whatever it is that we might call that guiding star in our life. I will never forget that moment when the outer world seemed to show me that I had disappeared. This experience informs my intense search to understand my own mind and how the brain-mind works.

The amazing brain-mind impassioned many others before me to undertake similar searches for understanding. In the 1600s, René Descartes, the influential French philosopher, mathematician, and scientist, questioned how a nonmaterial mind could influence a material body. He claimed that "mind and matter" were two different aspects of reality and therefore could have no relationship to each other. This entire book is a challenge to Descartes' notion. In actuality, the mind and the brain coproduce our lives, and the brain's miraculous evolutionary design created a mind-brain bridge by which the two interface and work with each other. It is the mind and brain together that produces conscious awareness. And the brain's ongoing evolutionary process of change influences all levels of awareness.

The brain has periodically taken dramatic leaps in both size and functionality to increase our conscious awareness. The last was around one hundred thousand years ago, when our brain doubled in size in a short period of time. The brain evolves so we can heighten our conscious awareness to "open out" or "unfold" into a better interface with our environment and to develop a wide diversification of new capabilities. This last evolution opened our brain to higher levels of objective thinking.

The mind is not located in any specific place in the brain and yet the mind is intimately involved in all the brain's activities. Neuroscientists' new definition of the mind is that *the mind is what the brain does.* To use an analogy, the mind is the CEO, in this case deciding what instructions to give to the brain in order to get things done in and through our bodies. For example, the mind holds the intention that you want to brush your teeth. The brain responds by sending messages through the nervous system to the muscles in the arm for you to reach for the toothbrush and brush your teeth. It is also possible for the mind to lead us astray, but it has the ability to reform itself. The mind can be retrained to change our habitual patterns, reduce stress reactions, and alter our attitudes, emotions, and outlook on life.

We play an intrinsic role in how we evolve our consciousness in this mind-brain interaction. Conscious awareness is determined by where we place our attention. In this chapter, we will examine what needs to shift in our attention in order to create an integrated consciousness. The first challenge to shifting our attention to achieve this state of wholeness is the chaotic culture in which we live. Our Western lifestyle puts enormous pressure on our body, brain, and mental response to the conditions of our lives.

Western culture is an intense, fast-paced, goal-driven, and competitive society. We have constantly to generate a lot of energy to meet its challenges. The demand for more energy occurs on all levels, not just in our work, but also socially and individually. In every area of our lives, we are driven. In addition to the demands to be professionally successful, we must also be rich and beautiful, have great sex, acquire the latest car or gadget, and go on exotic vacations. The culture keeps molding us into something other than what we naturally are. As a result, our desire to be successful tends to produce a great deal of emotional and physical stress. Few of us meet this standard of cultural success or become financially able to buy all that entices us, creating more stress. The problem for many of us is that the intensity of this drive to claim our place in the cultural hierarchy is the opposite quality of a mind that develops mental, emotional, and physical health.

There is an unconscious, silent stimulator embedded in our psychic core, a fear that keeps us in this chaotic cultural programming. Now the underlying driving force programmed by our DNA is to survive physically. This is normal programming for all organisms. But our mind can distort this natural survival instinct and focus our fear not only on the fact that we will die, but also that we will lose our ego, our individual identity, what we call the self, and be annihilated. We fear our nonexistence. This drive can get exaggerated to the point that it becomes survival at all costs. It is survival of me against you. We see how destructive this is to ourselves, others, and to the planet when it is expressed through competition, power, and war. More important, the ultimate cost to us is our own mental imbalance and physical ill health.

In teaching meditation over the years, I have seen this fear of death in participants in my classes and workshops. Some people are frightened to close their eyes or be silent even for just a few minutes. At the heart of this fear of the dark and/or of being quiet is the basic fear of nonexistence. When one gets cut off from the outside world, such as in meditation, it is easy to fall into fear-consciousness and to try driving away that fear by plunging back into the cultural soup of distractions. To confront that inner world, which is the real source of our greater identity and peace of mind, can be very fearful for some of us.

Sometimes the drive for success, or "being the best you can be," is deceptively called optimal performance and is described as the highest expression of our capacity to work, play, and use our full potential. This drive, as positive as it may seem, can get out of whack when it is only expressed in competitive survival or "getting ahead." It can easily be propelled by an unconscious desire to compensate for an underlying dissatisfaction or disconnection from the self. This strong desire to prove ourselves can sometimes disconnect us in relationships with coworkers, spouses, friends, family members, and our very selves. For many people, it creates agitation, disharmony, and suffering, which spreads throughout our lives and results in chaos, crisis, conflicts, and frustration.

While optimal performance strategies can sometimes prod us onward, it is easy to become myopic and self-centered if we don't examine what is really driving us. Our culture creates high standards for success that most of us can't meet. We need to let go of our unmet expectations and drives. We need a time to pause, to evaluate, and to become conscious and just be in the moment. A different question to ask ourselves is whether we can survive without being special, without being the best or having the most. The cultural performance drive can get locked into our brain circuitry. As I will describe later, it is possible to unlock our brain's wiring by "shedding some light" on it, as it were. The mind can break the hold of this automatic circuitry by being self-reflective. We can consciously rewire this drive and other negative behaviors using mental tools.

The question of attaining optimum happiness and health was no different in the time of the Buddha twenty-five hundred years ago. He called these desires to be somebody special, to be liked, and to be the best a form of suffering. Today we call it stress. We get stressed-out from feelings of helplessness and personal powerlessness, from physical tension, from negative self-image, when we lack a future and have a loss of initiative, and even from an inability to express ourselves clearly. All of these conditions and more represent our suffering. Buddha said that at the root of all suffering is the desire for things to be different from what they are.

The basic question we all strive to answer is: "What truly makes me happy?" Brain research has shown that we are wired for what we really want; and what we really want is peace, kindness, and happiness. It came as a relief for me to know that in our brain wiring is a potential for happiness. We will be looking at this potential as we progress in the book. The real question at this point is: "How did we get off the happiness track?" One way is in thinking that our urge for happiness will be fulfilled when our desires in the outer world are attained. But all this striving or chasing after creates the opposite of happiness. Eventually, we become disappointed with the results of our efforts.

The next question we need to ask is: "What is happening when I have everything and still feel dissatisfied?" In my case, something begins to shift in my body, brain, and mind when I ask this question. When I ask myself why I am unhappy, other questions arise, such as: "How can I shift these strong desires that drive me?" or "How do I remain peaceful in the middle of undesirable situations?" or "How can I reduce my growing stress?" We will examine how the physical body, the brain, and the mind can help answer these questions. But first, we need to start at the beginning and delve into how the brain and mind work.

Brain Formation and Neurons

The beginning for us as human beings is when the ovum from the female and the sperm from the male merge into a cell called the zygote. This divides repeatedly until a cluster of cells form what is called the morula. In fourteen days, a streak extends from the top to the bottom of the morula, right in the middle of this cluster of cells. This streak is our primitive spinal cord. From the embryo's most outer layer of cells, the nervous system is the first to develop. Other cells from the outer layer eventually form our skin, but they first fold inward to form a neural tube for the spinal cord. The idea that the outer cells become the inner cells is a metaphor for the inner and outer worlds as we define ourselves. At the very beginning of our existence as a forming body, we began to create the pattern of an inner and outer world. We will discover that this happens at all levels and later leads to our description of how the mind and brain work together.

As the embryo continues to develop, a swelling happens at each end of the spinal streak to form a primitive brain and a pelvis. These cells keep differentiating until you see little ears and legs and other organs. At this stage, pea-like structures develop on either side of the primitive spinal cord. These structures are called somites. They are energy cells that eventually proliferate into thirty-one spinal nerves and the organs that develop along the spinal cord. The primitive spinal cord is like the trunk of a tree and the somites are the branches. They give rise to the leaves of the tree, and our internal organs are the fruit of the tree growing off the spinal nerve.

Our brain and spinal cord are considered the central nervous system, but the fundamental unit of this system is the nerve cell called a neuron. The human brain has approximately one hundred billion neurons. Each neuron processes information and sends it to adjoining neurons and so on throughout the body. Their messages are either to inhibit or stimulate a particular organ or to initiate a specific action.

They do this via chemical and electrical processes. Neurons fire five to fifty times a second, and millions, even billions, of these neurons pulse in continual rhythm and harmony. The combination of millions of neurons firing and sending signals all at once produces an enormous amount of electrical activity.

Neurons only communicate with other neurons and do so without physically touching each other. Chemicals at the nerve endings jump across a small gap between the neurons called a synapse to send the messages forward through the network. Each neuron connects to about one hundred other neurons, creating a network of about one hundred trillion synapses. The chemicals in the synapses are neurotransmitters, peptides, or hormones. The combination of the chemicals and the electrical pulsations through the neuronal structure creates brain waves.

The Neuronal Pathways

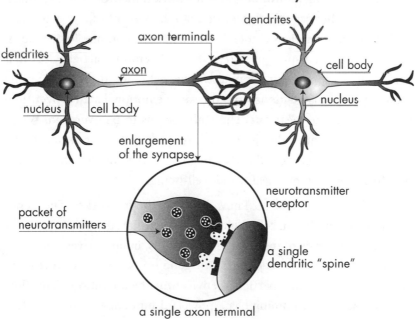

Brain Waves & Neurotransmitters

BETA: Dopamine	**THETA:** GABA
ALPHA: Acetylcholine	**DELTA:** Serotonin

When you clap your hands, for example, billions of synapses are activated together, repeatedly firing hundreds of times a second and creating an electrical current that can be detected by an electro-encephalograph. As the body's prime electrical generator, the brain constantly receives signals to create electrochemical reactions, which results in a flow of information to all parts of your brain and body. Neurons are changing all the time, as they do not have fixed proper-ties. The neuron grows axons and dendrites in less than two weeks. This allows for change and for rewiring to occur, thus giving us the ability of our own neural creation. This is the essence of our evolution. Neural construction is not seen in other animal brains.

As with all cells, the nuclei of neurons carry units of your inheri-tance—genes—and the chemical unit of your heredity—DNA. Genes encode enzymes to catalyze specific biochemical reactions in billions of neurons. Genes, or genetic inheritance and early life experience, shape the growing pathways of this network of neuronal connections. Some researchers say that no more than 25 percent of our emotional reactions are genetically coded. These genes contain instructions, however, that predispose us to repeat certain emotional behaviors that challenge or support our happiness as we get older. If the cells get the same repeated instructions from the same emotional states, over time our genes start to wear out. The DNA begins to be overused. When we repeat the same thoughts that are genetically connected to an emotional attitude, the cell's DNA begins to break down. The result is negative effects on our health and well-being.

Why do we need to know how our brain works? The genes encoded in our brain cells hold our inborn heredity traits such as behavioral patterns of instincts, natural skills, innate drives, tempera-ments, and sensory perceptions. Our gene traits are wired to react in distinct patterns under particular environmental conditions. This flow of automatic programming has a powerful influence on our habitual responses and reactions. These patterns seem impossible to change. But as we will soon see, the brain's neuroplasticity, or how it constantly changes, indicates that we can break old habits by releasing encoded traits and memories that are no longer useful. To change our automatic gene programming requires a mental training process of commitment, intention, attention, flexibility, and adaptability. This statement by Tibetan master Jamyang Khyentse Chokyi Lodro encapsulates the difference between the automatic and intentional processes:

> *The root of all phenomena is your mind. If unexamined, it rushes after experiences, ingenious in the games of deception. If you look right into it, it is free of any ground or origin. In essence it is free of any coming, staying, or going.*

The Brain–Mind

It is obvious that the brain and the mind work together. Most of us grew up with the notion that we are our physical body and came to identify that body as who we are. When we get sick, we focus on fixing or curing the physical body. We generally don't think about fixing our mind as part of the healing process. But the mind is very much tied into the physical brain. It is the mind that affects the body and can bring about healing and change in the body. The standard neuro-psychological view is that most, if not all, subjective, immaterial states of mind have a one-to-one correspondence with objective, material states of the brain.

Who gets you out of bed in the morning? Is it your body that moves on its own, or is it the mental intention that gets your body in gear? It is your intentional focus that directs the brain and through it the body. The brain-body does not work without the mind. As noted, *the mind is what the brain does.* It is the brain that moves neural information around, like the heart pumps blood. This means that the firing of the neural networking in the brain gives rise to mind information, and this is clearly observed in brain-wave patterns. Our mental capacities originate from the integration of the many neural circuits. These neural circuits run small amounts of electricity in our nervous system. If your body-mind is electrical energy, your mind has the ability to regulate and alter that energy.

Daniel J. Siegel, MD, professor of psychiatry at the UCLA Medical School and author of *The Developing Mind,* among other books, defines mind as a regulator of the flow of energy and of the flow of informational processing. For example, the flow of the mind's information refers to the meaning of the words you are reading right now. The flow of mental energy is also seen in the body's physical properties such as the tone of your voice, your alertness or sleepiness, or the intensity you feel in a relationship. When you hear a bird sing outside your window, what your ears hear is transformed into the mental sensation of hearing the song. When you cut your finger, the physical sensation in the body is transformed into mental-emotional pain. When you look at the color blue, the physical neuronal activity in the brain does not reflect the sense or feeling of the color; rather it is the mind that conjures up blue. These examples demonstrate that the mind acts on the physical brain to influence the electrical and chemical distributions affecting our perceptions and behavior. The mind stimulates the brain to fire, and over time ultimately changes the structural connections and networks in the brain.

The firing of neural networks in the brain gives rise to what we call the mind. The mind can be psychologically defined as qualities of thoughts, feelings, sensations, perception, attention, imagination, emotion, awareness, intention, and self-reflection. Each of these psychological characteristics can be found in specific areas of the brain. Also, the mind has mental activities such as memories that are physically found throughout the brain and in certain parts of the body. For example, when sitting in meditation, you can actually experience thoughts passing through your mind and then dissolving and passing out through various parts of your body.

This mind intelligence is actually spread throughout the body as well as the brain. In this mind structure and with all its functions, everything is connected to everything else, just as the network of neurons connects all parts of the brain. How the brain-mind interface works is still not fully understood. The scientific community calls this lack of understanding an "explanatory gap." There are parts of the mental process that cannot be explained by electrical currents and neurotransmitters in the brain. The brain just does not entirely explain the mind. Biologist and philosopher Julian Huxley said, "The brain alone is not responsible for the mind even though it is a necessary organ for its manifestation. Indeed an isolated brain is a piece of biological nonsense as meaningless as an isolated individual."

A practical way for each of us to understand and apply the brain-mind concept is to observe what we are paying attention to at any given moment. The Buddhists call this moment-to-moment attention mindfulness. It is a practice for learning to be conscious and aware of everything we do and say. The mind is organized to have this conscious awareness. We are mindful when we focus on someone through listening to or talking with that person, by physical touch, through feelings, or by inner reflection. We can also be mindful of internal physical sensations and the movement of our thoughts. These ways of being mindful can be experienced constantly throughout our daily lives. By being mindful of what is happening in any given moment, we can ascertain what state of consciousness is in control of our minds. It is this observing by the mind of what the mind is doing that provides a sense of choice. Do I want to express the anger that I am feeling? Do I want to listen to the bird singing rather than let my thoughts race madly in circles about a problem?

Each of us has the choice as to what state of consciousness we experience at any given moment of time. Do we want to be in habitual negative thinking and have stressful responses that are harmful to us? The mind has a huge impact on the brain and greatly affects our health and well-being. This mindful, aware, self-observing quality—the basis of meditation—arises from the fundamental way our brains have evolved. Neurologists' exciting discovery of the brain's neuroplasticity has radically shifted our understanding of brain-mind evolution.

Neuroplasticity

The repetition of electrical waves in our brain like ocean waves represents an incredible generation of power that can be harnessed for change. This potential for change is the magnificent breakthrough of the new brain research. It has only been since 1998 that scientists have discovered that "you *can* teach an old dog new tricks." Most of us have been told at some point in our lives that the way we are is the way we will always be. Well, this was never true. We now know that our brains do change, and we can consciously choose what new tricks we want to teach it.

The big news about the brain is that you can change the way you think and function. You can learn new things and develop new skills at any age. It was once believed that, as we age, the brain's neural pathways became fixed and thus unchangeable, that we were stuck with our aging brains as they became degraded over time. There is now strong evidence that the brain continues to evolve throughout adult life.

The new research has revealed that the brain never stops changing and adjusting. The phrase that neuroscientists use is that the brain has plasticity. This means it can change the size of different parts and alter functions as well as strengthen the connections between one area of the brain and another, just by how the individual mentally adjusts to experience. This means that the actions we physically, emotionally, and mentally take can literally expand or contract different regions of our brains, that is, pour more energy into quiet circuits and reduce activity in busy ones. The brain devotes more space to functions that are used more frequently and shrinks brain space devoted to rarely used functions. Thus, the adage "Use it or lose it" applies as much to the brain as it does to the rest of the body.

Technically, neuroplasticity refers to the changes that occur in the organization of the brain as well as an increase in brain tissue as a result of an individual's life experiences. The brain will sculpt and increase a tissue region in response to activity in our mental and physical environment. The brain changes not only in physical brain structure, but also in function, affecting the inner and outer environment. It is changed by the repetition of mental experiences, feelings, emotions, body states, and stress responses as well as changes in the immune system.

There are two ways to activate, connect, and grow neural networks. The first is by repetitive practice like working on a golf swing. The second is through having novel experiences such as taking an adventurous trip or learning a second language—any activity that is not routine. When we are actively involved in doing something new or that requires practice, the brain changes its structures and functions. When this occurs, the brain's nervous system fires its neural networks in response to this new stimulus. When neurons are activated, their connections to each other change and grow. In addition, supportive cells and blood vessels join them in the activation process. This is the means by which the organization and the volume of brain structures change.

To paraphrase Donald Hebb, a Canadian neurophysiologist and author of *The Organization of Behavior:* If neurons fire together, they wire together. This means that when two neighboring neurons are triggered at the same time on several occasions, the likelihood that they will subsequently fire in tandem becomes strong. They will tend to work together for a long period of time, developing more and more connections and neural networks. So that is how we increase neural "real estate" in the brain: repetitive action and novel experiences. It's great to know that the adult brain is not hardwired with fixed and unchanging nerve cells and networks. The power of neuroplasticity for growth and change is in effect as long as we continue to develop and use our mental capacities.

There are 1.1 trillion cells and 100 billion neurons that link to each other to sculpt the brain's experience. Each neuron connects to about one hundred other neurons to create a network of about one hundred trillion synapses. In ongoing research, there is a strong indication that new nerve cells may also grow. If you press your finger into a piece of clay, the clay has to displace itself to change form. This is what happens in the brain to accommodate a new skill, information, or procedure. New experiences, as well as those just imagined, mold the soft tissue of our brain.

In the mid-1990s, neuroscientist Alvaro Pascual-Leone conducted an experiment teaching a group of volunteers a five-finger exercise on a piano keyboard. He had them practice for two hours a day. After five days of this, scientists conducted transcranial-magnetic stimulation (TMS) scans on the subjects. He found that the size of the motor cortex had increased in the area of the brain related to finger movements. The scans of this area looked like dandelions on a suburban lawn. Pascual-Leone then took another group of volunteers who just played the piece in their minds, imagining how they would move their fingers to generate the notes on the music score. The results for both groups—those who actually played the piece and those who imagined playing it—were the same. Pascual-Leone concluded, "Mental practice may be sufficient to promote the plastic modulations of neural circuits."

Imagine changing the way you react to a situation in your life just by practicing the new ideal reaction! In this way, the brain is sculpted by pure mental activity. You can create a life of peace rather than one of anger, anxiety, or depression.

Can we really restore mental health by merely changing negative thoughts in a different but positive way? We absolutely can. Generating new and/or creative thoughts can change neuronal pathways, releasing the hold on us of old emotional patterns. The neuroplasticity of our brain gives us an opportunity to reshape ourselves to feel, think, and behave differently. The brain simply dials up activity in one region of the brain and quiets another. Altering neuronal connections may be the means to recover from trauma as well as open our capacity for love and compassion. In this way, depression or other anxiety disorders can be lifted. Brain sculpting shows that we now have the power to change our stress response. We can repeat a more healthy response and change the neuronal pathways reducing stress in our lives. It is amazing to consider that merely changing thought patterns could alter the very stuff the brain is made of and bring health to the physical body.

When we focus our attention on something, we activate the neural networks. The question that first interested me about this new brain research was: If learning a physical and mental skill can change neural networks, might meditation do the same? My answer came in 2006 when Dr. Sara Lazar did an experiment showing that meditation can increase brain-tissue size. She compared brain scans of fifteen non-meditators and twenty experienced ones—some who had meditated for a year and others for a decade. In her study, she had meditators mediate while the non-meditators just relaxed for about forty minutes a day. Lazar took brain scans of both groups during these periods. The results showed that the meditators increased the thickness of the brain's gray matter up to four- to eight-thousandths of an inch. The greatest changes in brain structure were from the ones who had meditated for several years and longer, with increases correlating to the increased length of time a person had been meditating in his or her life. There was no measurable increase of brain thickness in the subjects that did not meditate. What we are learning from the brain research is that when we focus our mental attention in a certain way, we activate brain circuitry and promote tissue growth.

Brain adaptability means that the brain is dynamic as opposed to fixed or static in its development. The brain is being modified throughout our life, and these changes can be both positive and negative. It all depends on what our minds focus on.

The brain has a sensory and motor strip across the top of the scalp. This strip receives and processes signals from points on the outside of the body from head to toe. These are touch sensations, visual and auditory perceptions, and kinesthetic systems that send nerve impulses to the brain. In one experiment, a monkey's thumb was cut. Months after the surgery to repair it, the region that processed those signals now came from the pinkie side of the palm and the back of the fingers. The brain structure that generally receives the thumb motor input had been coaxed to receive its motor input from a different brain region than that normally assigned to the thumb. In studies involving rats in which one area of the brain was damaged, brain cells surrounding the area changed their function and shape to take on the functions of the damaged cells. Such research has great implications for humans recovering from injury, surgery, and stroke. It demonstrates that we have incredible healing adaptability though the plastic ability of the brain to compensate for a lost function by shifting to another nerve-brain region.

Neuroplasticity also provides an interesting insight about happiness, which was previously thought to have a "set point" that cannot be changed. A set point means that we reach a point of intensity of happiness and cannot go beyond it. To some extent this belief was understandable because of the dogma that we couldn't change neural connections. It also implied that the wiring of the neuronal pathways in mental disorders was impossible to change. Researchers David Lykken and Auke Tellegen reported that the happiness "set point" could be changed. Though people tend to revert to their happiness set point, they can transcend it. Their research showed that, through practiced mental intention, people could remain unaltered and genuinely happy (positive, cheerful, balanced, etc.) in conflicting situations. The old view was that conflict would reduce a person's happiness. Through practice, a person can shift the happiness scale beyond what has been the so-called normal reaction. Remember that neurons that fire together wire together.

Richard Davidson, a researcher at the University of Wisconsin, has studied the effects of meditation on the brain. He has found that people who have meditated for many years can regulate their emotions in a more positive manner than people who withdraw and react negatively to difficult situations. His research tested meditators and non-meditators; both groups were asked to view emotion-provoking pictures. The results showed that meditators were better able to regulate their emotions in a more positive manner than the control group. The brain scans showed that they could shift out of a left-brain pattern during these emotion-provoking stimuli tests. There was also a notable increase in immune function in those that meditated regularly. Such research shows that mental training systems like meditation can reduce your stress patterns and improve your physical health.

The Mirroring Phenomenon

In the last decade, another aspect of the brain's adaptability has been discovered: mirror neurons. In Italy, researchers monitoring the brains of monkeys noted the neurons that fired when a monkey was eating a peanut. What surprised the scientists was that when the monkeys watched someone eating a peanut, the same neurons in that monkey fired, as if he were eating the peanut. Recently, these "mirror neurons" have been found in humans as well. This means we can mirror the brain activity of others. Mirror neurons in one person fire when that person observes a goal-directed behavior in another person.

I experienced a specific example of this mirroring when I was in a meditation hall doing walking meditation. I had been walking next to a man for about a half hour, when all of a sudden in my mind, I heard him tell himself to leave the room. I immediately turned to look at him, just as he turned, opened the door, and walked out of the room. My mirror neurons had picked up his intention. Our brains had been aligned during the meditation and his intention simultaneously fired mirror neurons in each of us. It also brought an instant of connection and understanding.

The brain is designed to be social, connect, align, and understand others. Remember the old saying, "Learn to appreciate another by walking in their shoes"? Mirror neurons enable us to actually do that. We respond to another's behavior or feeling or "read another's mind" all the time but are generally not conscious of it. Mirror neurons show us that we are linked on a level of mind where we can also feel an emotional resonance with people, which connects us. Mirror neurons allow the capacity for opening into empathy toward ourselves and others.

In a meditation circle I lead, I asked everyone to share an emotional issue that was current in their lives with one other member of the group. Those listening were to feel the same feelings being expressed by their partner. As the pairs took turns telling their stories, an amazing thing happened in the room. It became soft and quiet while the stories were being exchanged. What was created between each of them was a genuine love connection, a deeper relationship. In terms of what we know about how the brain works, both prefrontal lobes were engaged while neuronal networks were firing. (Note: In a neuronal network, the neurons are interconnected and influence each other in a kind of control loop.) Something was being felt and understood between these people that brought them into a deeper, more conscious way of interacting with each other. This type of conscious practice is how our brains consciously evolve and become more civilized.

When one begins to read and relate to another person's mind and emotions, it will no doubt increase our own adaptability and survival. For example, who does a small child emulate? They emulate their parents or caregivers, of course. The child imitates their behaviors, emotional reactions, attitudes, beliefs, mannerisms, and perceptions of the world. This was critical for early humans since tribal cohesion promoted survival. For us, having these traits programmed into our brains at such an early age explains why we often respond like one of our parents, or are triggered by a response that is out of context to our conscious values or beliefs. Our reactions to situations are wired at a very early age through mirror neural patterns, and these predetermined states of mind may persist throughout our life.

Dr. Joe Dispenza, featured in the movie *What the Bleep Do We Know!?* cites research indicating that we acquire 50 percent of our parent's neural network through mirroring behavior that is predisposed by our genetic inheritance. Then these genetic circuits are the platform on which we then build 50 percent of our personality through the experiences of our lives and through people who influence our programming via our mirroring them. This 50-50 mirroring split between genetic predisposition and environment raises some interesting questions. Whose thoughts are going through our minds? What is it to be an individual? Who are we really? The fundamental question with mirror neurons is: Do we actually transform our mind as we interact and mirror in our brain this relationship with others? Strange as that sounds, that is what neuroscientists say the mirror neurons do.

So how do we apply this neuroplasticity and mirror neuron research to becoming more conscious or making change in our lives? Research illustrates that as we focus our attention on our thoughts or emotions, reflect on ourselves, or align with another's inner world, the brain will create new neural connections. Neuroplasticity in itself doesn't create neural connections. It is through focused attention that brain growth and nerve integration occurs. Attention causes links to nerves from all over the brain and the body to build up new networks. Then, for some reason, these neural connections fire all at once. When that happens, a mental transformation or awakening to a deeper connectivity to ourselves and others occurs. There is literally a change in the way you see or experience the world. Learning to use neuroplasticity consciously is the key for mental-emotional balance and feeling fully alive, vibrant, and connected. The mental tools described later in the book are a triggering system for using the neuroplastic function of the brain. Together they work and allow us to evolve, change, and become more conscious.

The mind and the brain have distinct activities and functions in each of the three evolutionary brain structures: the reptilian brain, limbic system, and the cortex. Once we understand the different structures and their activities, it will give us insightful clues about our behaviors and ourselves. These structures also give us a map of how to train the mind. Utilizing the brain's neuroplastic and mirror neuron gifts, we can make positive and healthy conscious changes. To further understand how to use these gifts, we will now explore the organization of the evolutionary triune brain.

The Structure of the Brain

Neuroscientist Paul MacLean, MD, formerly of the National Institute of Mental Health (NIMH), developed a model of the brain's structure, which he called the "triune brain." He identified three parts of our brain: the neocortex or new brain, the limbic system or mammalian brain, and the reptilian or old brain. MacLean found that the human brain acts like three interconnected biological computers. He explained that each "bio-computer" has its own intelligence, subjectivity, sense of time and space, memory, and types of brain waves. The neural interconnection between the three is essential for us to function.

To visualize the three brains, think of each as a new addition on a house. Each new addition to the house alters the older structures to some extent.

What we find when we examine the brain is that one layer of gray matter was plopped on to another layer, and then the next on to that layer, moving from a primitive existing system to a more powerful one. The brain can be seen as an ice cream cone with different scoops piled on top of each other. The lower "scoops" were left unchanged as the other scoops were added in evolutionary jumps over many millennia. The bottom scoop is the reptilian brain, the middle scoop is the midbrain (limbic system), and the top scoop is the neocortex.

The Evolutinary Triune Brain

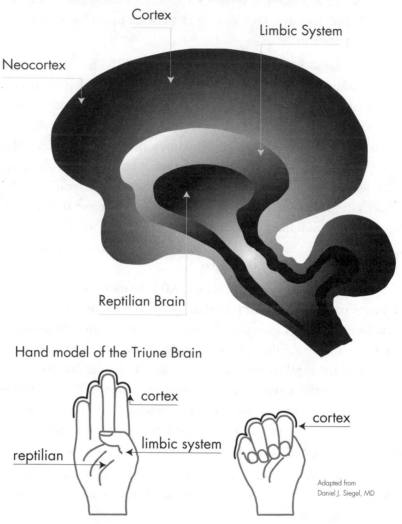

Cortex

Limbic System

Neocortex

Reptilian Brain

Hand model of the Triune Brain

cortex

reptilian

limbic system

cortex

Adapted from
Daniel J. Siegel, MD

Another way to visualize the structure of the brain is to use your hand. Open your hand and place your thumb inside your palm. Imagine your wrist being your spinal column that comes up into your neck. The base of your thumb and the palm of your hand are the brain stem, which goes up into the cerebellum and the reptilian brain. Your thumb placed against your palm is the midbrain or the limbic system. Your fingers are the neocortex or the new brain. Now close your hand over your thumb and look at your fingernails facing you. The two middle fingers represent the area behind your eyes. The two outside fingers are the sides of your forehead near the ears. The top of your bent fingers represents the top of your head, and the back of your hand is the back of your head. Using this model gives us a visual representation of the three brain areas.

We will explore the reptilian brain first because it is the most ancient part of the brain.

Reptilian Brain

This part of the brain (the bottom scoop in the ice cream cone analogy) took hundreds of millions of years to evolve. The reptilian brain is often called the "old brain." It consists of the brain stem and cerebellum (the wrist and palm in the hand brain model). It is called the reptilian brain because the basic instinct of a reptile is to "go for it" or "get away from it." It is a remnant of our prehistoric past and first evolved in lower animals. The reptilian brain experiences instinctively and reacts quickly to someone or an event, and it does so without thinking or making decisions. It is a triggered to react when we feel threatened or in danger. The reptilian brain is fear-driven and is our survival radar. It sees the world as survival of the fittest, and is territorial about getting food and keeping from becoming food. Act or react, fight or flight, or freeze. The reptile's concern is: "What do I eat, who do I mate with, or who will eat me?" The reptilian brain preserves our life moment by moment.

Our reptilian brain receives sensations about the outside world from all parts of the body and from receptors such as eyes and ears. This old brain is a kind of switch box, routing the sensory signals to the other parts of the brain. It appears that the old brain has a limited tolerance for turning off its control system, even when we are in a situation that requires a different focus. With the switch on, we pay less attention to our inner sensations than sensory input from the outside world. For example, you may be in a difficult emotional situation in which you are being abused emotionally. If the switch is on, you are not aware of your inner sensations and may not be able to make the best decisions for your mental and physical health. The good news is this "flaw" switch gets turned off as you become more conscious of yourself through the use of mind tools in mental training.

The reptilian brain is our automatic system. It regulates alertness, sleep, heart rate, and respiration. It generates survival strategies in tandem with the rest of the brain. Underneath our conscious awareness, this automatic system makes many decisions about our physical body. It plays a part in emergencies when, for example, an injury requires that more blood be routed to that part of the body, or extreme cold necessitates moving blood from the extremities to the vital organs. The reptilian brain alerts the neocortex to mobilize all systems in a quick and unemotional reaction to any urgent situation.

In humans, this old brain differs somewhat from the brain of a lizard, but we have retained the reptile's aggressive nature, territoriality, ritual functions, and social hierarchies. The reptilian brain operates in a patterned, habitual way and is by itself unable to alter inherited or learned behaviors once fixed in that brain area. In our daily life, the old brain develops learned motor skills such as those needed in playing the piano, driving a car, typing, or riding a bike. In this learning process, there is an interaction between the old brain and the new brain or neocortex. The neocortex helps the old brain observe and figure out how to improve the skill or increase performance. It is mechanical in nature in order to keep us repeating the same behaviors over and over again.

The reptilian brain is driven by three unconscious instinctual survival needs. One may be more dominant than others or may be more prominent at certain times in our lives. I've noticed that each of us usually has one instinct that is a "blind spot," or needs more work to make it accessible. With our reptilian brain, we all are somewhat unconscious of our strategies for a safe and protective life. Therefore, the first survival need is to attend to the basic practical life necessities. We protect ourselves (and our egos) by having enough shelter, food, money, investments, and physical comforts. With this survival instinct, we try to meet our work responsibilities, attempt to maintain our home, pay bills, and keep good dietary practices and exercise schedules.

The second survival strategy is an instinctual knowing that human beings are in themselves weak and can easily be taken over by antagonistic forces. With this instinct, we protect ourselves by being in an organized social structure, because we know intuitively that there is safety in numbers. In this strategy, we focus on relationships, knowing that it is important to have friends and to have interactions and connections in high and powerful places. Each of us attempts unconsciously to form a basic society or support system of people who provide some form of a safe community. This is most prominent when people work in organizations or in situations where they learn together. These conditions bring assurance, which takes care of the instinctual survival needs of the reptilian brain.

The third unconscious instinctual need is a driving force to experience intimacy with others. It may be for the reproduction of the species but also for a sense of increased energy and togetherness. People dominated by this instinct live their life as if they are a magnetic being pulled like a "moth to the flame." They feed on forms of energy that bring excitement and high levels of intensity. They are run by an unconscious need to connect with an exciting force that charges them from the outside. The drive of this instinct is to explore the world with intense inquiry and in exciting stimulation. These people carry an attractive vibrant energy, which drives them to seek intense intimate contact. This exploratory energy creates an intense union.

One of my clients provided an example of operating from the reptilian brain. A thirty-five-year-old corporate executive, he was considerably overweight and sweated easily in my air-conditioned office. He had not been sleeping, partied too hard, and was unable to get things completed at the office. These signs and symptoms are characteristic of the reptilian brain.

Limbic System

The limbic or mammalian brain (the middle scoop in the ice cream cone analogy) is the next evolutionary layer of the overall brain structure. Limbic comes from the Latin word *limbus* and means "edge." This part of the brain is a complex system of nerves and networks involving several areas near the edge of the cortex concerned with instinct and mood. It is also called the "emotional or hormonal brain." The limbic system layer controls the basic emotions (fear, pleasure, anger) and our drives (hunger, sex, dominance, care of offspring). It is what separates us from reptiles and what we have in common with other mammals: emotional bonding. It includes an important set of brain structures working together: the hippocampus, anterior cingulate, and the amygdala.

It is fascinating how evolution integrates the "old brain" into this new layer of the limbic system. Where the reptilian brain is focused on automatic body functioning, safety, and protection, the limbic adds something new and quite different: an intuitional state that is relational and emotional. The new brain tissue, folded into the "old brain," has made the reptilian brain more intelligent and flexible and shifted it toward the mammal's ability to "connect."

In our hand model, your thumb represents the limbic system. Notice that your thumb is connected to the palm and therefore still functions as part of the reptilian survival system. The limbic is about the size of an apricot, but it has a huge influence on our behavior. As such, it provides for a more socially oriented survival mechanism by developing in us the mammal's need to nurture our young and to connect with groups. The limbic also increases the intensity and range of our sensations of smell and hearing; therefore it raises our entire sensory system to a higher order of perception.

The reptile's life is simple: eat or be eaten. The limbic system is more complex and discriminating, particularly with the ability to nurture children and develop relationships. As the limbic system evolved from the reptilian, they joined together and developed our capacity to relate to the "other," not just to the self—to evaluate and relate to the other's emotions. The limbic system also regulates the expression of our emotions, as well as our emotionally charged repressed memories. And since memories relate to the past, the limbic system registers the past as well as the reptile's present time. There is also a remarkable dance between these two brains on how they relate to the outer and inner worlds. The two systems really do support each other. The reptilian brain is focused on the spontaneous sensations received from the outer world, while the limbic system gives an awareness of our inner world.

The limbic system adds a layer of emotional reactions to the reptilian brain's fight, flight, or freeze. This includes the emotion of fear in the survival response known as the "fight or flight syndrome" or "fight-or-flight response." The limbic system relates to a plethora of emotions that range from fear, pain, and rage to joy, peace, and love. It also introduces feelings of wanting to be the best or have the most, or be special or be liked. One of the emotional brain's functions is to avoid pain or unhappiness, so we learn to keep busy in order to repress negative feelings about ourselves. We do this by repeating experiences or becoming addicted to foods or drugs that produce pleasurable experiences. This behavior is generally rooted in a deep unpleasant feeling of unhappiness. As these compensating behaviors recur to mitigate negative feelings, the brain creates new neural networks to support them.

Each time we repress or express emotions, brain chemicals are needed for the information to flow. The limbic brain could also be known as a chemical or hormonal brain because it is a chemical-electrical network for the transfer of information. This brain structure has a strong influence on and regulation of the chemicals and hormones that affect our internal conditions. When the communication doors are open between the different brain structures, there is a flow of energy that brings emotional clarity to what we are feeling and what we are able to consciously express. When the doors are closed, there is a chemical backup that blocks the flow and affects our conscious awareness of how our emotions are affecting our health and happiness. (We will delve into this subject in chapter two.)

I have found in my work with clients that when the communication door between the triune brains is closed, most people are not aware of their feelings and what they want to express. Many people are frustrated or have an underlying anxiety about which they have no understanding. They blame others for their own emotions and feelings, rather than opening to those uncomfortable feelings. There are mind-tool practices that open the borders of the limbic to communicate down into the reptile brain and up into the cortex. Training the mind to become aware of how to open the border gates is the key to emotional change and health.

The three main areas within the limbic system—the anterior cingulate, amygdala, and the hippocampus—are involved in our emotional health and impact both the body and the mind.

The *anterior cingulate* is the bridge between the prefrontal neocortex and the limbic system. It connects our emotions with

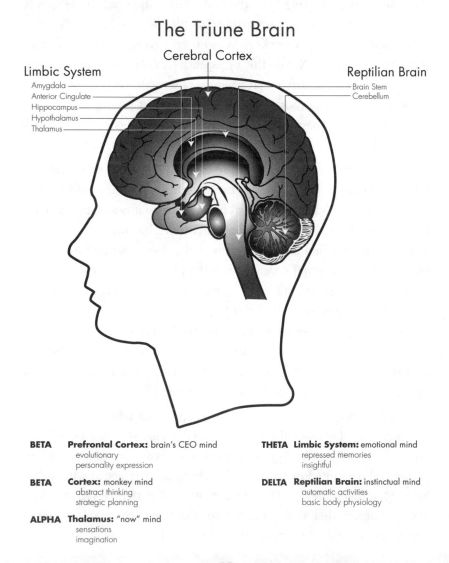

The Triune Brain

Cerebral Cortex

Limbic System
Amygdala
Anterior Cingulate
Hippocampus
Hypothalamus
Thalamus

Reptilian Brain
Brain Stem
Cerebellum

BETA	**Prefrontal Cortex:** brain's CEO mind evolutionary personality expression	**THETA**	**Limbic System:** emotional mind repressed memories insightful
BETA	**Cortex:** monkey mind abstract thinking strategic planning	**DELTA**	**Reptilian Brain:** instinctual mind automatic activities basic body physiology
ALPHA	**Thalamus:** "now" mind sensations imagination		

our cognitive skills, thereby playing a crucial role in emotional self-control, focused problem solving, and error recognition. Its value in mind training is to allow self-consciousness to emerge. The anterior cingulate is the CEO of the limbic system. Its purpose is to focus our attention, respond with empathy to another's pain, and regulate and monitor our perception of conflict. We use this focusing and regulation process constantly without being conscious of its impact. Imagine you are driving your car home on your usual travel route without paying much attention. You suddenly come to a detour sign. It is your anterior cingulate that alerts you to the changed route and the need to focus on driving.

The purpose of the *amygdala* is to scan all incoming stimulation in each moment and determine your level of safety. It drives such emotions as fear, sadness, aggression, joy, and anger. The limbic system processes these sensory streams and is involved in recording our earliest emotional survival experiences, what we learned in our first three years of life, such as touch a hot stove and you get burnt. This survival activity is below our conscious awareness, and it shapes the way we respond to situations. In infancy, the nerve cells in the limbic brain become wired together in response to sensory stimulation. The limbic brain does not mature as we grow older. When our emotional "buttons" are pushed, we continue to react to incoming stimulation as though we were two years old. This happens to us even when we are adults. The automatic reactivity of the amygdala can be rewired with mind tools, however, using the neuroplasticity of the brain to reevaluate the current situation and then purposely choose a more mature response.

Lastly, the *hippocampus* stores our emotional memories from three years old onward. It records our memories from each moment to the next and then transfers them into long-term memory. The primary focus of the hippocampus is survival and relationship issues. It also is linked to the body through our hormonal system and attempts to balance general body conditions, the immune system, and the autonomic nervous system. The latter governs the parasympathetic system, which applies the brakes to body functions, and the sympathetic system, which accelerates them.

Due to the brain's neuroplasticity, the limbic brain's negative emotional memory can be repatterned by changing the neuronal wiring of that memory with positive healthy reinforcement. The limbic brain can also develop interpersonal relationships as it provides a sense of self in relationship to another. When we put these relationship potentials together, we can repattern our brain and it can change our lives.

When the limbic system functions to support a positive focus and to heal negative memories, we have the capacity to develop more intimate relations with other people or with the natural world. A sense of appreciation of others and ourselves opens as the limbic system becomes conscious. A healthy relationship between the reptilian brain and limbic brain helps us to appreciate self and other, to find meaning, and to coordinate our motivational drives for survival. This dynamic will be pivotal in our discussion about conflicts, resistance, happiness, and using mind tools for change.

Cortex and Neocortex

The cortex, the largest structure in the brain, plays a key role in higher brain function such as thought and action. The cortex is highly wrinkled, which provides more surface area for neurons to function and increases its efficiency. This brain has twice the thickness and twice the functioning capacity of the other two brains. The cortex is divided into two parts or hemispheres with a thick band of nerve fibers called the corpus callosum between them. This acts as a bridge connecting the two halves and enabling them to communicate with each other and with the other two parts of the brain. If put end to end, the nerve fibers in the corpus callosum would stretch to the moon and back.

The neocortex is the fourth and latest brain structure in our evolutionary development as human beings, the top scoop in the ice cream cone analogy. Neocortex is Latin for "new bark" and this part of the brain can be likened to the bark of a tree. In the hand model of the brain, it is the top layer of the right and left cerebral hemispheres, the top part of your fingers and hand when you make a fist. The neocortex is divided into the frontal, parietal, temporal, and occipital lobes, each of which performs different functions.

This newest evolutionary part of the cortex evolved six layers to the external surface of the brain, gray matter that is filled with neurons believed to be what makes us uniquely human, what separates us from other mammals. These most recently added neurons create the circuits that give us our ability to think linearly and abstractly in symbolic systems such as mathematics, to develop language, and to observe activities objectively rather than reacting to them in a fixed emotional pattern of behavior. Beneath these neuronal circuits is the white matter, the wiring of which connects the different areas of the cortex to provide more area for the billions of neurons to operate.

The top three layers of the neocortex monitor the automatic thoughts of planning, memory, and decision-making. The lower three layers regulate our direct, focused experiences. For example, they monitor awareness of our breath and our feelings, as well as the ever-present interface of sensations between our body and the outside world. These direct experiences make us aware of being alive and having meaning and purpose in life. If the upper three layers of cells are too dominant, this keeps us from feeling alive.

In this third brain, our awareness also encompasses the future, along with the past and present focus of the other two brains. The neocortex gives rise to our personality and our individuality. Translating information from the outside world into imagination and thought allows us to form what we experience as an inner world model.

The new brain structure of the neocortex transfers information to the entire brain and body via predominantly beta brain waves and their chemical cohort, dopamine. These electrochemical impulses are fast in their vibratory movement (12–30 Hz), transmitting your past and future thoughts. When you close your eyes for a moment, you can recognize your thoughts intensely rushing through your mind, telling you what needs to be done, judging what you have done, and figuring out what to do. Beta gives the message that you are a busy individual engaged in the world, performing many roles and having many experiences. This new brain has been called the "monkey mind" with its fast-paced beta brain waves.

One of my clients did volunteer work. When I saw her, she had just returned from a weekend retreat with a board on which she served. She could not stop talking and her mind was going a mile a minute, jumping from one idea to another. She was activating the cortex of her brain and needed a relaxation method to calm her mind and reduce her stress.

The right hemisphere of the neocortex provides visual, spatial, imaginative, and holistic functions. It allows us to experience inner visualizations, scan our entire body, sense space around us, and create with our imagination. The left side provides the logic, linguistic, and linear faculties. This hemispheric intelligence gives us our verbal language, common sense, judgment, and our ability to think linearly. Through the corpus callosum, each hemisphere has a direct route of communication to the other. In a sense they talk with each other in different if complementary ways to give us our amazing, harmonic, and complicated capabilities.

In my opinion, the right brain is particularly important because of its link between the limbic system and the reptilian brain. This leaves the left side of the neocortex with no direct connection to emotional, heartfelt feelings or to the autonomic system. Generally, emotional thoughts travel from the limbic brain system through the right hemisphere and over to the left. This lack of direct connection between the left hemisphere and the limbic system may be nature's failure to knit our higher intelligence with our heart. When our "head"—our logical, abstract side—is cut off from our "heart" and positive emotions, we can act in a cold-hearted abstract way and not consider the consequences of our actions on others. In our complex and scary world, it is of great importance to integrate these two functions of head and heart for our future survival.

Integrating the creative and heartfelt tone of the right brain with the left-brain's abstract intelligence enables us to generate strategic planning, complex development patterns, and broad organization skills for the good of everyone. An emphasis on just the left-brain capabilities in our culture, which only value conceptual reasoning and rational judgments, diminishes in all of us the qualities of caring and kindness so needed in our complicated overstressed world.

Combining the two hemispheres also brings us the "what if" syndrome, or the curiosity to explore questions, problems, and possibilities of the unknown. Through the spirit of this inquiry, novelty is brought into being: the freshness of the new, the original, or the unusual. Our natural drive toward this kind of novelty helps us to evolve both hemispheres of the brain through neuroplasticity, which ultimately can evolve new behaviors and add greater diversity to our world.

It would seem obvious that the newest level of the brain would dominate the lower levels, but that is not the case. The neocortex and the limbic system have neuronal interconnections as seen in our hand model where the thumb actually touches the front fingers, representing the frontal lobe of the neocortex. With each new structure, the previous brain integrated its functions with the new brain in order to be compatible and supportive of the new. The limbic system demonstrates, however, that it can dominate or take over the neocortex. For example, can you remember being in an emotional state and how difficult it was to make a clear decision? Also, our reason is influenced by our constantly changing emotional and bodily processes, and can affect the neocortex's ability to function effectively. Our higher and more evolved new brain does not rule by itself. The social, emotional, and bodily processing of the other brain areas directly shape the abstract reasoning of the neocortex. New research indicates that by being conscious and aware of our emotions and then verbalizing the feelings aroused, the neocortex will make the connections and bring mental clarity. (In part II, we will explore this mental-emotional clarity via a particular mind-training practice.)

The working of the triune brain is highly complex. Neuroscientists are just beginning to scratch the surface in understanding its multifaceted nature. The three brains, although discrete in function, interact in ways that literally change each other. The way we experience other people, the world, and ourselves changes our perceptions. The really amazing discovery is that these perceptions and physical interactions also change the structure of the brain itself. It is this mutual process of physical and perceptual change that provides the basis for evolving our own brain-mind. Just knowing that every thought, attitude, emotion, and experience we have affects the development of our brain should motivate us to be more conscious of what is occurring in us every moment.

Prefrontal Neocortex

There is another important brain structure that greatly adds to the smooth working of the brain. Sometimes called the fourth brain, the prefrontal neocortex, which is situated right behind your forehead, points us in the direction of our next evolutionary leap as humans. The triune brain has been around for thirty-five million years of evolution. The three brains paved the way for the emerging development of this fourth brain. Approximately one hundred thousand years ago, the prefrontal neocortex emerged in humans in its present size as it appears today.

In the hand model, the prefrontal neocortex is the fingernails of your four fingers. The two middle fingers act as the CEO of the brain, which makes executive decisions for the other parts of the brain. Notice how your fingers all touch the other two brains by enclosing the thumb and the palm. The prefrontal region links the entire brain altogether as a whole. The two outside fingers in the model represent the part that regulates our working memory to influence our attention in the moment, and focus our planning and how to execute it.

The prefrontal neocortex offers functions that I call "the mind's tools for change." They can help the mind balance itself when used with our conscious awareness, intention, self-reflection, and focused attention. In meditation practices, they can create a communication link with the rest of the brain that stimulates resonance in the neuronal networks as they fire together in synchrony. This neural response has the capacity to shift our reaction to disturbing life situations and create harmony and health.

The prefrontal neocortex develops and grows rapidly immediately after birth, slows down, and then at age fifteen there is another rapid growth period in which it completes itself by our mid-twenties. This ends when this prefrontal region connects to every part of the brain; it now begins to regulate the growth of neural structures in the two hemispheres, and every gland, lobe, and region of the brain. This prefrontal region operates beyond the shortcomings and constraints of each of the other three brain systems as the leader of the whole brain. This executive function discriminates between choices like good and bad, consequences and outcomes, predictions and options, socially approved or non-approved behavior, and so forth. It is this area of the brain that gives us our direction in mind training.

The major evolutionary role of the prefrontal region is to upgrade and turn our unsocial reptilian brain and the emotional limbic system and us into a more social, cultural, and morally advanced being. As I personally see it, this newest brain development gives us the potential and opportunity to curb our suicidal violence and create a society of kindness, compassion, and love for everyone.

Richard Davidson of the University of Wisconsin, after doing the research on Buddhist monks who had meditated for many years, found greater mental activity in their left prefrontal neocortex than in their right. He identified this left region as the location of the new "set point" for measuring happiness in our lives. Davidson believes that happiness is a quality of mind that is literally located in this structure of the brain. His research demonstrates that it is possible to develop this area of the brain more fully through mental and physical practice. The Tibetan monks did this through sustained periods of meditation. Once developed, it is easy to return to this brain function for solace no matter what is happening in our life. This sheds new light on our real source of happiness. The external search for happiness, which all forms of media and entertainment promote, is incidental to the continual deep source of happiness that inner work can generate in our left prefrontal lobe.

Knowing how to develop this prefrontal area is the new frontier of brain research. In *The Mindful Brain,* author Daniel J. Siegel, MD, lists nine functions of the prefrontal region that strongly influence, and are also responsive to, neuroplastic changes resulting from meditation and focusing on positive life experiences. These functions are: regulation of body functions, emotional balance, social communication, mental flexibility, empathy, insight (awareness of self), regulating fear, intuition, and morality for the good of all. If we monitor our thoughts, it makes sense that this will help regulate our emotions. When the brain-mind flow is open, there is no fear in one's social expression. The development of an ethical life is then a natural result of kindness and a nonjudgmental attitude toward the differences between ourselves and others.

Brain development is like building a house. The foundation is the reptilian brain with its autonomic, sensory, and motor intelligence. The first floor is the limbic brain with its emotional capacity and relational intelligence. The second floor is the right brain hemisphere of the neocortex with its responsive imagination, creative, and spatial intelligence. The third floor is the left-brain hemisphere of the neocortex with the capacity of reason, analytical decision-making, and abstract thinking. Finally, there comes the roof, the prefrontal region, giving us the capacity to move beyond our automatic and unconscious conditioning. It lifts our habitual instinctual nature and awakens our mind to become more conscious and to take the next evolutionary leap in our development. This will take us out of conflict, self-limitation, immorality, and emotionally negativity. Each of us knows that these negative mental states decrease our health and happiness both individually and as a society. How we will make this evolutionary leap to allow the prefrontal lobe brain regions to flow and communicate with the rest of the brain and body is our challenge.

2

The Flow

Of what avail is it if we can travel to the moon, if we cannot cross the abyss that separates us from ourselves. This is the most important of all journeys. And without it, all the rest is useless.

—Thomas Merton

I wrote my first book, *When Sleeping Beauty Wakes Up: A Woman's Tale of Healing the Immune System and Awakening the Feminine,* out of compassion for people like myself who had become disempowered by a disabling disease (in my case, chronic fatigue and immune dysfunction syndrome [CFIDS]). I had an irresistible urge to motivate, to encourage, and to give hope to these people. My vision was to create groups of women in which women would provide support and healing for each other and themselves. I called these circles: Women Healing Women.

When my book was published, I felt a remarkable flow. Everything came together in perfect timing, with me connecting with the right people and making the right decisions about what I needed to do. The workshops and events I planned flowed like a stream of water without obstructions. There was nothing to interrupt its steady movement. I put on a major symposium for women; I developed an engaging presentation that combined acting, singing, and presenting of material that appealed to many types of groups and brought me recognition throughout the country as someone who understood their pain and suffering. When I appeared on TV shows or did radio interviews, I was a smash hit. The response was overwhelmingly supportive of my vision.

A group of people began to form around me. This group encouraged me to consider creating a health retreat center for people with CFIDS and similar chronic immune illnesses. I became magnetized by their enthusiasm and vision. I began to move into their vision and leave my own. When I began to leave off my own work and vision, doors began to shut, the stream got clogged, and I got stopped in my tracks. My energy started to decrease and my enthusiasm waned. The wonderful flow that I had experienced had totally stopped. When the flow stopped and everything seemed to crumble around me, I was devastated. Looking back, however, I see that the flow didn't stop. It simply began to go in a different direction for me, although it took me a long time to recognize it.

The word "flow" as I'm using it was popularized by the psychologist Mihály Csikszentmihályi and has been widely applied in many fields of investigation. Csikszentmihályi described Flow as a mental state in which a person is completely immersed in what engages her or him. The individual feels focused, energized, and totally involved. There is a merging of action with acute awareness. The notion of Flow has been a prominent feature of many spiritual traditions and is best represented by a sense of being at one with things. We can apply this concept to the flow of nerve impulses and chemicals in the brain and show how it affects our mind's focus and sense of attunement or flow.

In this book, I've examined how the brain has evolved into a complex structure that determines how our physical, emotional, and mental functions operate. The question at this stage of our exploration is: How do all the brain functions and the neural networks flow together optimally?

The brain's neural networks have patterned pathways by which they communicate information to each other. Imagine an event that grabs your attention and moves you to take positive action.

Electrochemical signals and neural networks send pulses directly to the reptilian brain to drive your action. Signals are received, processed, and sent to the limbic system, in this case generating positive emotional stimuli. These signals give rise to an emotional feeling that connects through neuronal pathways to the right-brain hemisphere of the cortex. The emotional and sensory input shifts across the corpus callosum to the left hemisphere, which processes it as a perception or a concept, or articulates it into words. It then moves from the left hemisphere to the prefrontal lobe, which coordinates and regulates the translation of information to the appropriate region necessary for use.

The Flow of Integration

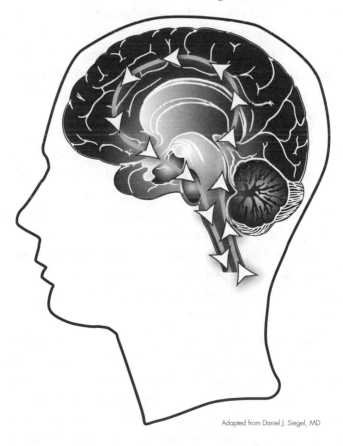

Adapted from Daniel J. Siegel, MD

If the flow of information across our brain moves in this manner in response to stimuli, we will have a flexible response and be rational in our thinking, self-aware and reflective in our thought processes, and intentional in our communication or positive in our attitude. That is how it all flows together on a good day. Of course, the outside event can be a conflict that triggers old memories, but the development of the prefrontal cortex allows us to choose how to respond in less reactive ways. Let's examine in more detail how this flow operates in our daily lives.

The Neurochemistry of Personality

In the nucleus of each neuron, lie our genes (the basic units of heredity) and DNA (the chemical basis of heredity). They incline us to develop particular traits such as physical features, attitudes, behavioral patterns, emotional responses, social roles, mannerisms, and what we call our personality. Neural pathways carry messages from our genes via electrochemical impulses to express our personality in the form of emotional responses and interests, for example. We identify with our personality traits; they are what give us the sense of being a person as opposed to merely a body with a brain. In addition, we are raised by our parents or other caregivers whose attitudes, beliefs, and behavioral patterns we imitate, incorporating their characteristics into our personality structure. We begin to imitate them by using our mirror neurons at approximately two years of age. Between our gene coding and using mirror neurons, we develop our distinctive personalities to make up what we call "me." Every thought, perception, sensation, cognition, and emotion that expresses this "me" has both an electrical impulse and a chemical component.

We wear our traits so closely that they are what and who we are. As we easily act out these traits over and over again, they become habitual, an electrochemical addiction. The chemicals in the neuronal pathways that have been reinforced by our repetitive behavior keep us "addicted" to the same pattern. For example, if you like things to be straight and orderly, you may believe that you acquired this naturally. Actually, your mind and its thoughts have reinforced this sense of orderliness from a very early age and this trait is a pattern of chemical and electrical impulses that gives comfort and familiarity.

Now, what if someone comes to work in your office or home and is constantly messy. Assume that they are just the opposite of you in maintaining an organized, clean space. You will most likely have a negative emotional response to their messiness and to them. What actually happens is that this person messing up your space disrupts your familiar and comforting neural flow of orderliness. The result is a surge of negative emotional reactions to both the situation and the person. This triggers your brain to release emergency chemicals to prepare for the defense of your orderly view of things. These chemicals pour into the bloodstream, triggering feelings of anger, fear, or anxiety.

At that point, the situation becomes a stress response triggered by someone else's patterns that are different from yours. You are now unhappy, anxious, or fearful. You want things to be different from what they are, so you react. Now, if nothing is done to change this negative response, it can continue and turn into you constantly raging against messy people. This raging against messiness now becomes familiar, and over time you get addicted to the chemicals that are released in the bloodstream. You get the picture.

These chemicals act like any addictive substance and keep us locked into automatic emotional behaviors. It is like being constantly asleep to what is actually happening to us. This is similar to someone who is in physical or emotional pain and takes heroin to cover the pain and feel pleasure. The heroin triggers the electrochemical flow of the neurotransmitter dopamine that will induce feelings of pleasure in the brain-body. Both the external substance and the internal reaction create a physical-emotional response.

We are a chemical plant that gets activated by automatic thoughts that keep us reacting to life. This automatic pattern of our thoughts, emotions, and actions stops the brain flow and creates a kind of deadness in our lives. When the brain is in a natural flow, we are conscious of the automatic and habituated processes that all too often drive our lives, and are poised to change them. Unconscious habituation can make us feel that life is meaningless, with little direct control. Without conscious thought or attention, we feel imposed on and often become a victim to what life brings us.

On the positive side of a neurochemical "addiction," chemicals are released when we experience romantic love. Helen Fisher, an evolutionary anthropologist at Rutgers University, says that the rush of exhilaration of passion is also a chemical addiction. People passionately in love describe sleepless nights, loss of appetitive, and feelings of euphoria. With romantic love, the brain is stimulating its reward center that governs obsession and restlessness. Stimulating this center creates feelings of romantic love. It is the same for cocaine and heroin addicts. They also repeatedly seek the intense pleasure that the drugs give them. It is interesting that the same neurochemicals, serotonin and dopamine, are released in passionate lovers and cocaine addicts. An interesting aside to the experience of romantic love is that while in the throes of this passion, the amygdala (our fear protector) in the limbic system is deactivated. When this stimulation finally runs its romantic course, you might wake up and wonder who this person is that you just married. Is this why there are so many divorces? Ponder this when you have your next romantic adventure.

In my younger years, I had the tendency to be a love junkie. I was single for fourteen years after my first divorce and a girlfriend and I said that we dated so many men that we could fill the Cow Palace (a stadium in San Francisco). I believe this continual overstimulation, this continual activation of the neurotransmitters dopamine and serotonin, might have contributed to my eventual burnout with chronic fatigue. I was looking for external happiness rewards (discussed in more detail in part II).

The Buddha called this automatic reaction pattern "suffering." He said, "I teach one thing. There is suffering, and there can be an end to suffering." As I said earlier, the modern-day term for this suffering is "stress," with which we have all become very familiar. We are so engaged with stress that we hold tight to physical and emotional tension and its pain without even realizing it. More important, we generally don't know how to identify and then reduce or change our sources of stress. Conscious awareness that stress is controlling us is the first step to changing and ending our suffering.

Stress responses can create a negative loop in our body-mind interface that keeps repeating itself over and over. There are two ways the brain responds to our reactions: via the nervous system and via the endocrine system (chemical system). Later we will look at how our personality types can also keep automatic conditioning and thoughts in place, and how our habitual emotional responses can be changed or transformed by a shift in how we use our mind. First, let's examine how stress affects us physically and mentally.

Stress and Your Body Systems

Internal flow gets stopped in two ways by the nervous system. One way is by something that externally threatens you. For example, you are walking down a mountain trail, and suddenly a brown bear jumps out in front of you and stands up on its hind legs. Do you run away, do you stand still and hope it moves on, or do you fight to defend yourself? Or take another example. In the middle of the night, you wake up because you smell smoke. Then you see the flames and feel the heat from your burning house. Your life is immediately threatened. What do you do? Do you try to save the dog first, or do you jump out of the window?

In these examples, flow is stopped through a physical experience that generates an internal reaction. The block can also come solely through your thinking. Imagine you are staying at an exclusive hotel and are to present an important paper at a conference the next day. All of a sudden at two in the morning, you wake up coughing and feel that you are coming down with a cold. You ask yourself, "Do I have a fever?" You think, "I bet I won't be able to present my paper tomorrow." You feel tightness in your chest and realize that you should have turned off the air conditioner. The anxiety begins to build until you are convinced that you have pneumonia. "Should I go to the emergency room before this gets out of hand?" And then more fearful thoughts rack your mind. "Maybe I can't find someone to take my place at the conference." These thoughts begin to build on each other until you are an emotional wreck from your own internally generated fears. This is when your imagination is not your friend. The reality is, you don't have a cold, but in just a few minutes you created an illness and axed a great career opportunity. There was no objective evaluation of your condition. Internally generated anxious thoughts combined until you imagined a crisis where none existed.

When the Flow stops from either external threat or internal imagining alone, the prefrontal lobe is closed down by these intense emotions and repetitive thoughts. Researchers call this top-down processing because internal information—the repetitive emotions and thoughts—assaulting the prefrontal lobe is stronger than our normal experience of the world and therefore blocks it out. At this point, it is difficult to think clearly, or respond emotionally in a healthy manner. We get stuck and can't see another's point of view, or can't even listen to ourselves. Let's examine what actually happens in the nervous system to stop the natural flow.

When an emergency survival situation triggers the fight-or-flight reaction and stops the Flow, the reptilian and limbic brains, which govern the autonomic nervous system (ANS), kick into action. The ANS has two branches. One is the sympathetic nervous system (SNS), which is involved in the fight-or-flight response. The other is the parasympathetic nervous system (PNS), which is involved in relaxation. Each system works in reverse of the other in order to keep a balance or to maintain homeostasis in the brain-body.

In our two earlier examples, with the external threat of the bear and the purely mental sickness, the sympathetic nervous system's alarm was set off in both cases. It is so named because it has sympathy for us when there is an emergency. The alarm signal originates in the brain, gets sent down your spine, and branches out into nearly every organ, blood vessel, and sweat gland in your body. It affects all these areas to prepare you to take coordinated action. At this point, adrenaline is released, and you experience all the symptoms of your body preparing for "fight or flight." You feel anxious and tense and, with the adrenaline flow, experience a heightened sense of perception. The SNS core response is to get your muscles charged up, as they need energy to act. One of the hallmarks of the stress response is the rapid mobilization of energy from storage sites throughout the body. The heart rate, blood pressure, and breathing rate increase in order to transport nutrients and oxygen at greater speeds through the body. Proteins are released, and fats pour out of fat cells into your muscles to support your survival. The immune system puts immune cells into circulation, releasing lymphocytes to fight off a foreign invader (microbes or other pathogenic organisms) or protect us in case of injury.

During an emergency, in addition to accelerating certain functions, the body inhibits others to conserve energy. Thus digestion is inhibited, growth and tissue repair is curtailed, and sexual drive is decreased in both sexes. When stress becomes chronic, females are less likely to ovulate or carry pregnancies to term and males begin to have erectile dysfunction and secrete less testosterone.

After the emergency has subsided or the chronic situation lessens, the PNS, the other half of the autonomic nervous system takes over to restore normal operations. Central to the operation of the PNS is the vagus nerve with its branches exiting from the brain stem and regulating structures in your head, face, digestive track, and heart. It plays the opposite role of the SNS in that it maintains homeostasis in the body. Thus it keeps us calm, promotes growth, stores energy, and keeps us optimistic. It would be a disaster if both systems were active at the same time. It would be like putting your foot on the gas and brake simultaneously.

Stress also affects the endocrine system, which is made up of glands that secrete hormones into the blood, the body's chemical messengers. This system is slower and less reactive than the nervous system, but can likewise shift us out of the Flow. The chemicals in our body move information from one network of cells to another. Hormone levels are influenced by stress and other factors as they move through the blood. Among the glands secreting hormones are the hypothalamus, thyroid, adrenals, pituitary, pineal, pancreas, ovaries, and testes. Other glands such as sweat and salvia are also significant in the stress and relaxation responses.

When under physical or mental stress, the neural networks of the limbic brain secrete a peptide (a chemical messenger) called corticotropin-releasing hormone (CRH). CRH then moves its chemical message to the pituitary, which releases adrenocorticotropic hormone (ACTH). ACTH travels all the way down the spinal cord to inform the adrenal glands that it needs to release a variety of steroid chemicals called glucocorticoids. These chemicals alter the internal world of the body and the mind, putting a stop to normal body maintenance functions. As stress hormones accumulate in the cells, the functions of repair, building, and healing decrease and the aging process increases. Therefore, the more you hold on to conflict, worry, and anxiety, the quicker you age as the stress hormones become locked in the cells and cause a deconstruction of the mind and body.

Stress is anything that throws the body out of balance. It can be the physical stress of an accident, injury, or harsh environmental conditions; a chemical stress from exposure to toxins, pollutants, or chemicals; or emotional/psychological concerns about a job or money, the loss of a loved one, health, or relationships. Anxiety is usually the first emotional alarm warning us about stress. The signs are hypervigilance, apprehension, and excessive worry. Anxiety is generally a diffuse, vague, and dreadful feeling. Fear, by contrast, is experienced when a particular object of focus triggers a negative reaction.

Another stress alarm is anger, which can be expressed by active or passive behaviors. In the case of active emotion, the angry person lashes out verbally or physically. When anger is passive, it can be characterized as silent sulking, passive-aggressive behavior, hostility, and tension. There are also emotional reactions that are a blend of positive and negative emotions. The positive emotions can make you alert, motivated, inspired, or stimulated. The negative ones can leave you concerned, uncertain, unfocused, and confused. For example, when your mother comes to visit, you can enjoy being with her while at the same time feeling the stress of extra work and responsibility.

Research indicates that women handle stress most effectively by caring for their children and finding support from their female friends.

Women's bodies make chemicals that are believed to encourage these responses. Oxytocin is one that has a calming effect during stress. This is the same chemical released during childbirth and is found at higher levels in breastfeeding mothers, who are believed to be calmer and more social than those who don't breastfeed. Women also have the hormone estrogen, which boosts the effects of oxytocin. On the other hand, men have high levels of testosterone during stress, which blocks the calming effects of oxytocin and causes hostility, withdrawal, and anger.

Once the stress emergency is over, the endocrine system goes back to its business of cellular restorations, repair, and reproduction. The nervous and immune systems return to business as usual as well. But when the body is continually flooded with stress-related hormones and our behavioral reactions keep repeating the stress stimulus, we have chronic stress. Our bodies are not designed to live under long-term stress.

For the first thirty minutes after the onset of an emergency situation, your system works for you at full force. The brain has an internal timer to stop the body's stress response after an hour or so. But what if the anxiety or fear continues? More stress chemicals are released and our body becomes overrun with them, resulting in more fears and anxieties. Sound familiar?

Many stressful situations don't provide an outlet for relaxation so that the stress chemicals can be released and flushed out of your system. These chemicals have nowhere to go and keep circulating in the bloodstream. Research has found that, if stress continues beyond the sympathetic nervous system's basic response time of thirty to ninety minutes for dealing with emergency situations, the continual exposure to high levels of stress hormones lasts from three days to two weeks. There needs to be an outlet to release these stress chemicals. A doctor friend of mine says, "Cells need to poop." We know that relaxation provides release, but all too often how we unwind and relax creates even more stress. The body's reaction to stress takes a lot of energy and vigilant attention. When it is chronic, it opens the way for disease to take root.

We can be suffering from stress when we are indifferent, worried, fearful, angry, upset, irritated, frustrated, jealous, hurt, impatient, anxious, agitated, suspicious, or just plain bored. Joe Dispenza, DC, says, "It takes one thought to change the degree of acidity in our stomach's secretions. Without ever moving a muscle, we can cause our pancreas to make hormones, alter our adrenal glands' hormones, get our heart to pump faster, direct our blood flow to our legs, change our rate of respiration, and even make ourselves more prone to infection."

The Effects of Chronic Stress

The following are some of the ways that stress affects the physical body when stress remains at high levels over a long period of time.

- **Energy** is continually diverted for the ongoing stress response, which reduces stamina and increases the risk of chronic fatigue and diabetes. The stress response drains the protein and fat storage sites as it funnels nutrients into fat cells, converts amino acids to sugar, and in the liver turns sugar into glucose. Also, your muscles and cardiovascular system never get a chance to be repaired.

- **Immunity** becomes compromised, increasing the incidence of bacterial and viral infections. Infection susceptibility rises and disease healing slows when CRH levels rise.

- **Digestion** is affected by an excess of CRH, which can result in irritable bowel syndrome. Mental disorders, phobias, and panic attacks create disturbances in the digestive process.

- **Blood pressure** is chronically raised so that your heart beats faster or irregularly.

- **Tissue repair and growth** are constantly being turned off, interfering with the development and repair of your body.

The brain is also affected by stress. Here are some of the effects:

- **Energy** is diverted from the brain so that the mind becomes foggy and cognition is unclear.

- **Memory and learning** are affected, as continually high levels of CRH result in the shrinking of the hippocampus region of the brain, which houses memory and learning.

- **Neurotransmitter** function is compromised by high levels of CRH.

- **Toxins** attack the brain due to high levels of CRH changing the blood-brain barrier that is normally not permeable by toxins.

The following are some of the ways stress can affect an individual's mental state.

Depression can result when the brain senses high levels of CRH and stops secreting it. But after ninety minutes or so, if the levels continue to rise, the feedback system fails to shut down and CRH accumulates, resulting in a chronic illness. The Flow has stopped. This alters and depletes the brain neurotransmitters: dopamine, which provides pleasure for sex and food; norepinephrine, which alerts the brain to provide physical responses to stress and panic; and serotonin, which aids in sleep. Depression arises in the emotional limbic system. It is a powerful force of pain and fear, and if you focus your attention on it, more chemicals are released to feed the depression.

We now know, however, that we can build a bridge from the emotional to the thinking brain through neuroplasticity. In *Mindfulness-Based Cognitive Therapy for Depression,* Drs. Zindel Segal and J. Mark Williams cite their findings that half their depressed patients with a history of repeated relapses did not fall back into depression after they used a particular mental technique for observing their thoughts. The doctors instructed their patients to regard their thoughts as fleeting transient mental events that come and go through the mind. The patients came to regard their thoughts not as reality but as butterflies floating into their field of vision. The doctors found that only half of these subjects fell back into depression after learning this technique.

Posttraumatic stress disorder (PTSD) can result from a lower base level of CRH but a high level of adrenaline during and after the trauma. Adrenaline is the memory imprint and acts like a photographic fixer. It floods the brain in a dangerous situation, creating an increased focus. Alertness and vigilance sharpen the mind to deal with the danger. This is the reason for the strong memory "flashbacks" of the trauma. Research has found that people with PTSD have symptoms of dissociation and have a smaller hippocampus in the limbic brain. They also have problems associated with memory, learning, and space and time orientations. Dissociation is breakdown in memory recall and can lead to a disintegration of sense of self. PTSD victims are likely to suffer from other disorders such as depression, alcohol and drug abuse, and a variety of phobias.

Obsessive-compulsive disorder (OCD) patients fixate on objects and activities, such as repeatedly washing their hands, checking and rechecking to see if the door is locked, and counting cars. Recent research has demonstrated the healing of OCD through neuroplastic changes in the brain from self-directed and repeated mental practice. Psychiatrist Jeffrey Schwartz, MD, of the University of California at Los Angeles, discovered in his work with OCD patients that the disorder affects two areas in the brain called the worry circuit. It becomes overactive and, in a repetitive negative loop, keeps bombarding the rest of the brain with feelings that something is wrong.

Schwartz thought that there must be a flaw in the brain wiring for the neurons to overfire or overreact in this way. In a ten-week research project, he proposed that a change in the brain circuitry would occur when OCD patients practiced observing their thoughts as if they were happening to someone else. They also imagined standing outside their minds observing their thoughts. He theorized that they would not see the flaw in themselves and would not react to their thoughts. The results showed a significant improvement in the patients' reactions. The repeated OCD behavior and the activities in the brain were dramatically reduced. The will and conscious effort of the patients altered their brain function, changing the brain chemistry and circuitry.

Aging is accelerated by chronic stress. The stress chemicals collect and circulate continually in our brain and body, resulting in the degeneration of the hippocampus, which is the center for learning and memory. Chronic stress results in compromised function of the CRH feedback regulation in the brain as we age; the brain fails to make the necessary adjustments when the chemical levels get too high or too low. In addition, as we get older and are not as active, our repressed automatic thoughts become more pronounced. When we are busy and active, we don't have time to dwell on them. The result is that these repressed emotional memories come to the surface of our conscious mind and capture our attention. If we are not using some kind of mental training, the rush of anxiety caused by past memories increases, as do the associated brain chemicals. Riding on the memories, anxiety, the stress hormones, and the changes in brain chemistry accelerate the aging process and produce depression. I think this is why so many elders become depressed.

Your Stress Level

Statistics about stress seem to confirm that the activation of our automatic thoughts and reactions are leaving a negative mark on society today. The real problem is that we fail to identify the true source of our stress, instead blaming everything from the president to the neighbor's barking dog for the tense state in which we find ourselves. We don't realize that, in fact, we are the culprit, that our stress stems from our social programming and our automatic reactions. Take a look at some facts about the impact of stress in our lives. I hope this will encourage you to be concerned and take action about your own level of stress. The mental training in part II of this book offers you practical ways to do just that.

Information from the Centers for Disease Control and Prevention (CDC) and the National Institute for Occupational Safety and Health is startling:

- Job burnout is experienced by 25–77 percent of U.S. workers.

- Employee stress is recognized as a major drain on corporate productivity and competitiveness.

- Depression, only one type of stress reaction, is predicted to be the leading occupational disease of the twenty-first century, responsible for more lost work days than any other single factor; 33–35 million U.S. adults experience depression in their lifetime.

High-pressure work environments take their toll on workers' morale, and many workers say they need help in dealing with stress. Working with a difficult coworker or overbearing boss elevates the stress levels. Computers, e-mail, and cell phones all increased the pressure to be more productive. Technology's reach has become a problem. The same tools that allow us to communicate more quickly with coworkers can now follow us home, on weekends off or on vacation, never allowing our bodies to rest and dump those stress chemicals. As workers suffer from health issues, the employer picks up the tab in higher insurance costs and lost productivity and passes it along to the consumer in higher prices. Too much stress will result in poor decision-making, ruined professional and personal relationships, and deteriorating physical and mental health for a vast host of workers, from the factory floor to the executive suite.

The first signs of stress usually develop slowly until surprising us with their negative impact. Since we have discussed stress chemicals and the effects of such hormones as adrenaline on our hardwired brains, it important to recognize the first signs of stress. It is critical to monitor your own stress level. Here are some red flags to give you a heads-up that you may be under stress. *Physical symptoms* include: weight gain or loss, digestive troubles, chronic high blood pressure, racing pulse, frequent headaches, insomnia, muscle fatigue and aches, teeth grinding, tension, neck and back pain, increased caffeine or tobacco consumption, diarrhea, fatigue, lack of concentration, and lowered resistance to colds and flu. *Mental symptoms* include: difficulty concentrating, short temper, low morale, sadness, depression, anxiety, frequent nightmares, rapid mood swings, irritability, feelings of isolation, and loss of intimacy with loved ones.

The following stress check can be helpful in determining your stress level.

Life Stress Test

This is a list of stressful events in life, each of which has an assigned rating indicating the level of pressure it adds to your life. In the past two years, which of the following major life events have taken place in your life? Add the points for each event to determine your total life stress score.

_____ 100 Death of spouse

_____ 73 Divorce

_____ 65 Marital/relationship partner separation

_____ 63 Jail term

_____ 63 Death of close family member

_____ 53 Personal injury or illness

_____ 50 Marriage

_____ 47 Fired from work

_____ 45 Marital reconciliation

_____ 45 Retirement

_____ 44 Change in family member's health

_____ 40 Pregnancy

_____ 39 Sex difficulties

_____ 39 Addition to family

_____ 39 Business readjustment

_____ 38 Change in financial status

_____ 37 Death of close friend

_____ 36 Change to a different line of work

_____ 35 Change in number of marital arguments

_____ 31 Mortgage or loan over $30,000

_____ 30 Foreclosure of mortgage or loan

_____ 29 Change in work responsibilities

_____ 29 Trouble with in-laws

_____ 28 Outstanding personal achievement

_____ 26 Spouse begins or stops work

_____ 26 Starting or finishing school

_____ 25 Change in living conditions

_____ 24 Revision of personal habits

_____ 23 Trouble with boss

_____ 20 Change in work hours, conditions

_____ 20 Change in residence

_____ 20 Change in schools

_____ 19 Change in recreational habits

_____ 19 Change in church activities

_____ 18 Change in social activities

_____ 17 Mortgage or loan under $20,000

_____ 16 Change in sleeping habits

_____ 15 Change in number of family gatherings

_____ 15 Change in eating habits

_____ 13 Vacation

_____ 12 Christmas season

_____ 11 Minor violations of the law

_____ **Your Total Score**

    This scale shows the kind of life pressure that you are facing. Depending on your coping skills or the lack thereof, this scale can predict the likelihood that you will fall victim to a stress-related illness. The illnesses range from mild (frequent tension headaches, acid indigestion, loss of sleep) to very serious (ulcers, cancer).

Life Stress Scores

0-149: Low susceptibility to stress-related illness

150-299: Medium susceptibility to stress-related illness. Learn and practice relaxation and stress management skills and a healthy lifestyle.

300 and over: High susceptibility to stress-related illness.

* Reprinted by permission of Dr. Tim Lowenstein, Stressmarket.com

---

By now you understand the need to train your mind to stay in the Flow: to lower stress levels, become healthier, more productive, live longer, and find peace and happiness. Part II will teach you how to use brain-wave frequencies to balance your brain during meditation as well as other easily implemented mind tools to promote equanimity in your everyday life.

At this point, let me summarize some key points about the evolved brain covered thus far. Most of us take this complex magnificent brain of ours too lightly. How blessed we are to have this 650-million-year-old brain that helps regulate our behavior and the automatic functions of our bodily processes, and from which our mind or conscious self has evolved with its unique ability to alter the brain where necessary to heal ourselves.

- The brain and the mind are coproducers of who we are. They work in harmony as the brain does what the mind intends.

- Mind-training research is now used in conventional medical circles to develop brain potential and to provide accelerated healing. This brain-mind investigation is truly a revolutionary movement for the betterment of humankind.

- Science has found that your personality is located in the prefrontal lobes of the neocortex, and personality disorders can be healed by altering this brain region.

- The research about thinking reveals new neurological insights. For example, each thought is transferred as information via your neural networks. Nerve cells communicate these thoughts by electrical impulse, with neurochemicals forming the bridge between cells throughout the body.

- The personality seems so real to us, but when science breaks it down, we see that our cells are communicating with each other and transmitting information in an automated machine-like manner.

Self-reflection and mind training is the way to break the negative pattern of automatic thoughts.

- As you learn to meditate, deep insights will gently rise you're your consciousness, bringing clarity and understanding. This is a direct clue to why mind training is so fundamentally needed in our lives. With meditation, your mind naturally becomes calmer, less reactive, and less personal. Through mind training, you can change your brain and ultimately your behavior.

Negative thoughts and desires affect brain evolution.

- The Western culture in which we live entices us to attain more stuff and do more things. This wanting affects our attitude, behavior, and experience, which in turn nega tively affects the growth and development of our evolutionary brain.

- Our brain is not fixed, as we have discovered, but rather changes with each novel experience, mental practice, and new thought. Mind training shows you how to be aware of the quality of your thoughts and experiences, or the way you focus your mind.

- Meditation research shows that when you practice a sustained breath meditation, you naturally develop a more positive, flexi- ble, and healthier state of mind. This practice will have a positive effect on your health, and most of all, this positive state actually helps grow your brain.

- When you grow a positive brain, you become more conscious and express a higher evolutionary state of kindness, empathy, and emotional balance. This evolutionary brain also brings a new morality of compassion for self and others. This developed morality can be a major impetus for constructive change in our world.

- Mind and brain training can be a major contributing factor to the brain's evolutionary process. Mind training is a way to shift this world from conflict and devastation to one of caring where we have a compassionate mind for all people and nature.

As we pay attention to a positive thought, it grows our brain.

- The recent discovery of mirror neurons demonstrates how compassion is developed in the brain. They prove that when we pay attention or imitate other people's positive behavior, we grow our brain. This in turn accounts for our own positive behavioral change.

- When you gently gaze into the eyes of another and feel that person's feelings, it is as if those feelings are your own, and vice versa. The result is you both "feel felt." This mutual reflecting builds the brain to a higher evolutionary state. This is the reason for the concentration exercises of mind training, which develop your ability to focus your mind in a direct, conscious manner.

- Focused attention releases you from your negative automatic thinking and enables you to move past your struggle of strife and suffering. This state of release is what is called "Buddha Nature."

Your mind and brain are actually wired to give you peace and bliss.

- All of your one hundred billion neurons spread their messages constantly and continually throughout your body. The nervous system is the first "organ" we develop, and it continues to serve us in this capacity until the end of our lives. This wiring needs TLC in the form of practice, attention, experience, and conscious awareness.

- The brain has developed in a series of evolutionary leaps. The process started with the reptilian brain with its survival instincts and added the limbic brain with the mammal's emotional group orientation. Eons later another layer of brain bridged the two sides of creative and linear thought in the neocortex. With this new brain, we are capable of evaluation, discrimination, and discernment.

The most recent brain structure, the prefrontal lobe, integrates all brain-mind functions.

- The prefrontal lobe regulates the flow of nerve impulses to your bodily functions, maintains emotional balance, and allows you to self-reflect.

- This brain structure gives you the ability to focus on and change what doesn't work in your life and in the world. It allows you to gain insight from what you have learned and to apply it for constructive change. It also opens the deep compassion within you to show empathy to yourself and others.

We have an epidemic of stress in our culture that takes its toll in widespread pervasive suffering.

- To discover what short-circuits your potential to be peaceful, you must understand how stress can stop the body-brain-mind flow both physically and mentally. Stress has very distinct signals that eventually become noticeable through obsession, depression, and anxiety disorders. Chronic stress continually floods our system with a variety of chemicals that make our suffering habitual.

We can use our brain's capabilities every moment of the day. What we need to ask ourselves is: What is the route to unleash my brain-mind gifts? What opens my creativity to express the qualities that can change my experience of the world? The answers to these questions lie in the use of mind tools to become aware of the brain frequencies, qualities, and imbalances. This awareness serves as a map to guide you in achieving brain synchrony, which we will explore in depth in the next chapter.

3

Whole Brain Synchrony

Through our presence,
we will create a refuge where dignity can be restored,
where our preciousness can be discovered,
and where we can mend ourselves
in places that are broken.
It is here that we can dream the dreams
that make all things possible

—Ronald W. Jue, PhD

There is a story about the Buddha and a prominent scholar. This scholar would go from village to village speaking about the sacred texts. One day he heard that the Buddha was in the next village, so he decided to go and hear him speak. As he came into the listening circle of people, the Buddha looked up and spoke directly to him. The Buddha told the scholar, "You remind me of a man I once knew who counted cows. Every morning as cows in the village went out into the pasture and every evening when they came back for the night, the man counted them. This man had never milked a cow, never owned a cow, or even touched a cow."

"How is it possible that I remind you of such a man?" the scholar asked.

The Buddha replied, "Because you have never experienced what you are teaching. Isn't that true?"

"What do you mean?"

The Buddha asked him, "Have you ever experienced the oneness of being, the expansion of multi-universes, or have you ever been in deep stillness or in deep peace?"

The scholar shook his head and said, "No, I have not."

The Buddha said, "Please join my sangha of monks and be in silence with us for two years." The scholar accepted the Buddha's invitation and became a monk. Two years later the Buddha called him back and asked the former scholar if he had any questions.

The scholar said, "I have no further questions. I am at peace."

I tell this Buddha story to indicate how important our direct experience of meditation is in discovering true inner peace. We can attain a lot of information about what meditation is, but if we don't have a direct experience of our inner world, we will never have true knowledge. It is said of shamans that they don't know that water is made up of hydrogen and oxygen, but they know how to make it rain.

Many people have observed that knowledge combined with experience is what creates wisdom. Wisdom about our lives, our purpose in life, and how to live with grace and freedom comes from self-reflection on what we have experienced and what we know. To be truly wise we have to learn how to integrate our knowledge and experience.

When you become a student of your own mind (as you will in part II), you peel back the layers and make your way layer by layer to that inner place that brings a sense of calm, peace, and aliveness as well as a sense of connection. You become like the sparrows with their speed and unpredictable flying pattern that venture far away but always know how to come back to their nest.

One of my clients reported such an experience when she first started to train with me. One day she was in a big "funk." Her mind was scattered, and she was unable to focus on her writing or anything else. She could feel in her body that something was wrong. She became so uncomfortable with this anxiety that she went into her backyard and meditated. Within a half hour, her mind became quiet as she reached what she called a "sublime state." The anxiety and tension in her body was gone. She felt centered and in harmony with the world around her. As she came back into the house, she noted how happy and clear she felt, and for the rest of the day, every moment was enjoyable. She was like a sparrow who found her nest, a place to rest her mind and to come home to her whole self. So let's look at how we can find that home, our own little resting place.

The writer Anne Lamott once said, "My mind is like a bad neighborhood [and] I don't want to go there alone." If you have never taken time to observe your mind, you may be under the impression that it is calm and quiet. If you watch your mind moment by moment, however, you will likely be astounded at how difficult it is to keep your attention fixed on one thought.

Let's experiment with observing your mind. Wherever you are sitting, stop reading this book. Look around and pick some object to focus on for a moment. Just look at it and hold your attention on it, then return to reading this book.

Did you notice all the thoughts that "popped up" as you tried to focus on the object? For most of us, it is extremely hard to keep our attention on something and not have a stream of thoughts flooding our mind. In a very real sense, we never fully see the object itself. Rather we form a mental conception of the object that we hold in our mind—our previous experiences with similar objects, naming them, our evaluations, judgments, and so forth. In various spiritual traditions, the mind is often referred to as a "drunken monkey." The busy-ness of day-to-day experience intrudes, and as a result the mind becomes scattered and unfocused. Again, stop reading and take a few moments to close your eyes and note the stream of thoughts and images as well as bodily sensations that flood your consciousness.

In those few moments, you probably noticed the jumble of thoughts and vague impressions that arise so quickly it is difficult to track their continual chaotic flow through your consciousness. If you observe them for a few minutes, you will also discover different categories of thoughts all moving through at the same time. Some thoughts may be emotionally charged, like recreating past events. Others may reflect exchanges with people, plans that need to be made, or movies and television programs you have watched, and so on. The mind becomes excited, agitated, and distracted as it induces you to make plans or engage in evaluations and judgments. Before you realize it, you are scrambling down these rabbit holes of thought and slip into absent-mindedness. After the exciting activity from this flow of thoughts depletes neurochemicals, the mind naturally moves into a slower, sedated or tranquilized state. This is the vagueness that you may have felt when your eyes were closed. This is when we become bored and the mind becomes lazy and dull. In this state of mind, we readily become the proverbial spaced-out couch potato as our minds become dull and lethargic and lack direction and focus. We have basically hypnotized ourselves and have gone into a self-induced trance state.

These two states—an overstimulated mind and a lethargic one—seem to be inherent in all of us. There is a tendency to continually swing from one state of mind to the other, creating in us a lack of centeredness. What is most challenging is that we have little or no control over these two movements. This unconscious pushing and pulling between mind states not only affects our thoughts and feelings, but also influences our physical reactions and responses. It is easy to understand why the prison system puts criminals in isolation with only their minds for company. To be isolated from people in a bare cell with no distractions is severe punishment for those with chaotic minds. Boredom, loneliness, fear, and depression can overwhelm those without mind training.

I have always been amazed at the negative response from people when I talk about my long silent meditation retreats. What is clear is that most people find solitude very upsetting and scary. The most common response is "I could never keep quiet for a day, let alone for three months!" My secret is that, by applying mind-training tools, solitude became a wonderful gift, freeing me from the chaotic nature of my mind. We all want to be free from inner turmoil and confusion, and I am committed to guiding people to discover for themselves that they can become more peaceful. Thus, by learning and practicing some simple tools, your mind becomes open to creativity, you have a clearer place in which to make decisions, and you discover a refuge of inner peace. The first step is to learn how to work with your brain and mind in order to become more conscious.

This process is not new; what is novel is our modern scientific approach. Many religious traditions through the ages have explored how to work with the mind. In monasteries in both the East and West, we have the writings of monks and nuns who devoted their lives to spiritual practices and meditation techniques that transformed their minds and led to a wide range of mystical experiences. Many of these writings, such as those by the Western mystic Saint John of the Cross, describe in detail the altered states of awareness that they explored. Buddhism has probably been the most methodical in providing specific techniques and pathways to attain certain states of consciousness.

Modern science now has the technology and research capability to map how consciousness actually arises in us. This mapping both validates many of the meditative religious traditions of the past and shows us consistent pathways to discover from a variety of methods suitable techniques for developing our brain functions and mind states. Knowing our unique brain patterns will help us overcome dysfunctional patterns as well as open to us a range of possibilities for expanding our consciousness. First, let's examine how the mind works to change the brain.

Changing the Brain

In actuality, the process of changing the brain is quite simple. The conscious intention of our mind when used with focus, attention, and practice can restructure the brain and change its functions. The mind can vary certain functions of the brain by changing the rate (speed) and amplitude (power) of the electrical pulses in the brain. We can alter our behavior by changing these electrical pulses. Like playing the piano, we can play our mind-brain in such a way as to produce well-being, happiness, and bliss. Through diligent practice, a mind can become more aware and consciously awake. The mind, if focused, can be a very powerful force. Yet most of us play around with some parts of the mind and leave vast regions unexplored.

In the work of changing the brain, we want to explore all the dimensions of the mind to find our most integrated state of consciousness. Like people who have learned to mentally play the piano just by reading the music, you are going to learn how to shift your mind from discord to harmony by becoming more conscious. Changing your mind is not just a psychological experience, although that is certainly part of it. This mind shift actually changes the brain physically. If you recall Richard Davidson's research on the Tibetan monks, discussed earlier, he established that the mind (through meditation) trains the brain to physically grow and change itself. His experiments measured actual increases in brain size and activity that occurred in the left frontal cortex.

Let's come back to the concept of Flow. When you are in physical and mental Flow, there is a communication networking or a joining together of all levels of the brain orchestrated by the mind. It is these brain interconnections that create a vibrant, alive, and aware mind. Earlier we observed how unconscious automatic stressful thoughts and emotions obscure this dynamic Flow within us. Recall the example of when you wake up in the morning and hear a bird's song. In a very short time, a whole committee of automatic thoughts begins to interfere with this beautiful greeting. They grab your attention, tell you to get ready for work, plan to take the kids to the soccer game in the afternoon, and get food for the weekend outing or call a friend who just had surgery. The committee sends these messages so fast you can't even take a breath.

With a trained mind, however, you will be aware of this mental activity, but rather than being overwhelmed by it, you can just smile and continue to enjoy the bird's sweet song in the moment. This being aware but letting go of the thoughts and keeping your attention on the singing is a conscious mind choice. You choose to refocus, let thoughts settle, attend to the moment. When you do, there is a calm centered awareness as you move into the Flow. You will see that the techniques, methods, and practices to evolve your brain-mind consciousness simply help to create intention and to focus your attention on certain regions of the brain so that the mind can naturally heal itself through the brain's neuroplasticity.

Brain Waves and Brain Structures

In my studies of the triune brain, I found that each of the three structures have different functions, behaviors, speeds, and chemistry. I understood how this applied to mind training when I learned about the work of Maxwell Cade, a British psychobiologist and biophysicist. Cade grew up practicing Zen meditation. In the 1970s, he conducted research programs examining the brain waves of many healers and advanced meditators. He was determined to find easier ways to enter into these "advanced states" of mind, and used an electroencephalograph designed to show immediate brain rhythms from both sides of the brain simultaneously. He called this electroencephalograph a "Mind Mirror." For years, Cade used the Mind Mirror to observe advanced meditators. From his Zen training, he knew that the first step in the art of meditation is to have mind-body awareness. This simply means turning one's attention from one's thoughts to focusing on bodily sensations. As in most Buddhist and Hindu practices, focusing on sensations like the breath quiets the mind and gradually develops higher consciousness and awareness.

In his research, Cade investigated how the brain responded when someone was in an altered state of mind. He found that this state of consciousness was built on an integrated pattern of electrical brain-wave activity. He called this integrated state an "awakened mind." Cade was able to demonstrate in his research that this awakened "meditator" mind is a specific combination or signature of the four brain waves: beta, alpha, theta, and delta.

My research has been directed toward discovering such brain-wave signatures in stress profiles and sometimes in trauma. As I noted earlier, stress is anything that throws the body out of balance. Chronic stress patterns such as high anxiety are usually accompanied by an imbalance in one of the brain structures as revealed by its corresponding brain waves, such as beta waves for the neocortex. These signatures can be used to correct behaviors that reflect mental and physical imbalance. I also use the measurement of chemical neurotransmitters in the brain as another indicator of which brain wave is involved.

In my work, I use the Brain Mirror, which is another electroencephalograph that gives a visual display on a computer screen of brain-wave patterns in various states of consciousness. The value of a monitoring tool like the Brain Mirror is that it can show the range of a person's meditative state and how to balance and stabilize the mind in everyday life. It can also reveal the brain-wave signature of highly stressed states of mind, which allows a trainer like me to help the client repattern and change the affected brain structure and function. This alteration is then reflected in the client's attitudes, behavior, and life changes. As I watch the brain waves on the electroencephalogram (EEG; the recording), I can imagine the brain-wave patterns as a visual image of what the neurons look like as they are firing in tandem or in synchrony.

When a person is hooked up to the Brain Mirror and given feedback while in an awakened state, this seems to imitate the experience of being mirrored by another person, which activates the mirror neurons, as discussed previously. The same process can be used with

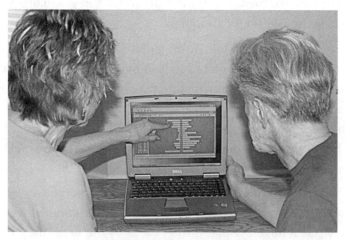

Don viewing his brain waves on the Brain Mirror.

imbalanced stressed states of mind such as chronic anxiety or addictive behavior. Once we've discovered the specific causative pattern of brain waves, these can be repatterned to shift the person out of this state. The mirror neurons will imitate the feeling and body experience of this mind state and enable the person to repeat the mind state experience at will, or, as in our example, shift out of anxiety.

Here is an illustration of the process. Don came to me to learn to meditate in order to reduce his anxiety about issues with his boss. We first had a conversation about the extent of his tension. I then placed electrodes on his head to hook him to the Brain Mirror and measure his brain-wave activity. I was able to see the brain-wave activity on my computer as I took him through a procedure of questions, exercises, and meditations related to each brain-wave function.

His high amplitude of beta brain waves and delta brain waves indicated his stress pattern. This pattern indicated the type of meditation that would work best for him. I played the brain-wave activities from my computer for Don to show him his patterns. The Brain Mirror is a remarkable teaching aid.

Then I took him through a Beta Relaxation Meditation so that he could see the difference in his brain-wave response. I instructed Don to use this meditation daily and to do it with the Relaxation Meditation CD. The CD is an important training tool to begin to reduce stress by rewiring the brain. He needed the practice to change the neuronal patterns and to use the mental tools to handle the stress stimulants that have controlled his life.

From my introduction to Cade's research on brain waves, I launched into an intense study and exploration of the new research emerging on the brain. I also began to study the interrelationship of brain waves and what types of meditation practices best suit individuals, based on what their natural brain pattern shows. (I later expanded this research to include the effects of specific stress trauma patterns on state of mind as well.)

The Buddha was said to proclaim that there are eighty thousand ways to meditate, meaning, I believe, that there is no one right way

to meditate. There are, however, specific approaches to mental training that can activate and awaken clearer states of the mind and heal
unclear ones. As I studied each brain wave and the brain structures
from whence they derive, I gained more insight about how I used my
mind and where I placed my attention, or how to pull myself back from
dissonant states.

Scientific research is showing that mind states act as a symphony, with each brain-wave frequency playing its own characteristic
part. Each type of brain wave has specific qualities and correlates to a
certain brain structure. Each wave pattern and the affected structure
add their own unique piece to the puzzle of a person's distress and how
person is blocked from experiencing other states of consciousness.
Any EEG shows how consciously a person naturally uses brain waves.
When an EEG demonstrates flexibility, that is, the ability to move
quickly from one type of brain wave to another, the individual will be
able to experience the different consciousness states and use them to
impact his or her evolving brain.

The four brain-wave frequencies—beta, alpha, theta, and delta—
exist in a rapid pulsation in relation to each other. The relationships
between these frequencies shape our thoughts, behaviors, and emotions. Becoming aware of the various levels of consciousness that these
brain-wave patterns elicit allows us to expand our awareness and to
heal and balance our lives.

Before we begin to explore mind-training techniques, it would
be helpful to have some technical background on the four brain waves.
Each level of the brain has a brain-wave pattern produced by tiny
electrochemical pulses of varied frequencies. Brain-wave activity is
recorded in the range of 1–50 Hertz (Hz), which is a unit of frequency
representing the number of cycles per second. In my practice, I do not
generally encounter the frequencies from 38 to 50 Hz (gamma waves),
but I will talk about them later in the book. The higher the hertz, the
faster the frequency, and these faster frequency patterns are predominantly in the neocortex of the brain. Thus a higher level of information
processing tends to generate more beta frequencies (13–38 Hz). Also
in the neocortex are alpha frequencies (7–13 Hz). In the midbrain

are the slower theta frequencies of the limbic system (4–7 Hz). The reptilian brain primarily generates very slow delta frequencies (0.5–4 Hz). Thus our states of consciousness can be measured. The electroencephalograph is able to read the electrical potential that is liberated by the neurons that send messages between the brain regions and the body. (Note the overlap in hertz between the brain-wave types. Moving from one to another is a gradual frequency shift.)

There are also four neurotransmitters that correspond to the brain waves. Beta is associated with dopamine, alpha with acetylcholine, theta with GABA (gamma-aminobutyric acid), and delta with serotonin. The purpose of neurotransmitters is to communicate information between neurons and their neural networks in order to process information. As described earlier, the nerve endings release chemicals when the electrical pulsations of the brain waves go through the neuronal structures. Brain waves and neurotransmitters are primarily produced in specific locations in the brain, but researchers have discovered that these neuronal connections are experienced in every part of the body, not just in the brain.

To help you remember which type of brain waves are generated in which brain region, it might be useful to recall the hand model of the brain. Your fingers represent the neocortex and beta waves, your knuckles the parietal lobe of the cortex and alpha waves, your thumb represents the limbic system and theta brain waves, and the palm of your hand is the reptilian brain and delta waves.

The RAS and Consciousness

The brain regions with their electrochemical signals do not, of course, work in isolation. Rather, these brain structures connect and relate to one another in interconnecting neuronal networks and electrical patterns. The functioning of the brain stem and cerebellum of the reptilian brain generates the delta brain waves and the serotonin neurotransmitters. This electrical-chemical interaction in the brain stem provides us with an incredible gift. A cluster of cells (about the size of your little finger) between the brain stem and the medulla in the reptilian brain is called the reticular activating system (RAS). The

RAS is enormously important because it wakes you up in the morning and puts you to sleep at night. And it plays a major role in developing consciousness. The cortex cannot function unless the RAS is in an aroused or awake state. Without this function, we would not have an ability to think, perceive, or respond to stimuli. The brain cortex cannot wake itself up; what awakens the cortex from sleep and keeps us awake is the RAS.

Consciousness is impossible if the RAS is damaged or destroyed. It is believed that the cortex and RAS operate in a feedback mode, the purpose of which is to maintain an optimum level of wakefulness. Simultaneously, when electrical impulses carrying sensory information reach the cortex, they are routed to the RAS. And when the level of stimulation becomes too high, the RAS sends back messages to the cortex to reduce the stimulation. On the other hand, when the stimulation is too low, the RAS sends messages to increase alertness.

Most of the functions of the reptilian brain have an automatic program. For example, if you want to move your arm, there is no need to decide which muscles to use. This part of the brain also controls our automatic reactions (of which we are completely unaware) to other people and situations. In the limbic system are stored habit patterns based on fixed beliefs, which may be irrational, ungrounded in reality, or inappropriate and self-defeating. We usually don't deal with them because of the flaw in the reptilian brain mentioned earlier and how it routes sensory signals that keep us focused on the external world. We are unconscious of behavioral patterns. The brain responds to a program or reaction imprinted from a traumatic situation by repetitive conditioning, or like an automatic gear, we keep repeating a destructive response over and over again.

To stop destructive behavior, we can learn to use our minds to stimulate the RAS and make the brain-mind more conscious about what is happening in our interior world. We can immediately start up the RAS by turning our attention inward as we become more self-reflective. When we do that, our mind becomes quiet and we begin to connect with an inner knowing as to what the right decision is for our lives. It is through cooperation between the cortex and the RAS that self-regulation is achieved. The RAS can be trained with its inhibitory connections to work with the cortex and help it stay in balance. Chronic and anxious reactionary states interrupt this flow of communication, however, and shut down its positive functioning.

When anxiety intrudes into the brain-mind system, it impairs both the communication pathways and the chemical functioning of the brain. These dysfunctions can result in a decreased ability to think clearly and act from an inner focus. In the reptilian brain, dysfunction may be expressed as insomnia, sleep disorders, depersonalization, social and sexual disorders, eating disorders, moral laxity due to survival issues, lack of common sense, depression, and moodiness. Mental health problems such as obsessive-compulsive disorder, posttraumatic stress disorder, schizophrenia, and panic disorders are all thought to have their roots in the out-of-balance reptilian brain.

The RAS is the foundation for meditation and mind training, as it is the biofeedback loop between the cortex and the RAS that allows us to achieve conscious awareness to regulate our responses. When we react less to the outside world and are centered within ourselves, then the magic begins. Once our minds are lifted from the prison of fear and anxious response, there is a freedom of choice that can reduce long-standing automatic programs. It is clear from my experience both personally and professionally that the RAS can be trained in this manner.

When my client Alice came to me, she was incredibly anxious. She had just been summoned to court by her former husband who wanted to stop alimony payments. She would have little to nothing to live on if the judge ruled in his favor. Her survival was at stake. As we worked together in rewiring her brain through meditation, she was unsure the process would work. But at her next appointment, her whole demeanor and attitude had shifted. She told me: "I now know that I am able to handle whatever the judge decides." Her anxiety had lifted and she could make clear decisions. She realized that she had reserves and potential to continue life in a new way without the alimony payments.

The reptilian brain also has the ability for selective attention. For example, when a baby cries in the night, the mother immediately wakes up to attend to its needs as the father sleeps. This instinctual part of her brain, always in a survival readiness mode, is also aware of her baby's needs. This selective attention allows us to narrow the inner and outer stimuli so that our minds can become stable and alert. When a mind becomes stabilized, it no longer jumps from thought to thought. This reduction of the "monkey mind" happens only with stable selective attention.

When my mind becomes stable in meditation, I get a heaviness or pressure on the top of my head and my awareness drops down through my body to become even more relaxed, free of pain and tightness. I become aware of subtle vital energies moving in and around me, that I am in a vastness outside normal time and space. As I drop into this consciousness, I find that my mind is attentive, bright, and alive. The mental sharpness of this mind state brings stable selective attention that is pristine and still. In this state, your brain can receive, classify, and respond to sensory information without the data interfering with or disturbing your state of consciousness. If you were to repeat this mental practice on a daily basis, you would be in continuous conscious awareness of the inner and the outer world simultaneously. Once the RAS is activated and makes its connection with the cortex, the unconscious becomes conscious. This fundamental brain function has the greatest impact on the changes and shifts in awakening consciousness.

Let's now look at what happens when the reptilian brain is running its channel of connection to reach the cortex and passes through the limbic brain. As the electrical pulses from reptilian brain connect with the midbrain or the limbic system at the top of the brain stem, these two brains interface closely with each other. It is imperative that the cortex and the reptilian brain keep their communication doors open. They must constantly exchange messages for mental alertness, sleep functions, and involuntary body functions, and process sensory messages passing from the inside to the outside of the body and back again. To keep this interchange flowing, one of the limbic system's tasks is to maintain and balance the body's hormonal functions. The hypothalamus is involved in these functions and must be in balance for these exchanges to work properly. The RAS in the reptilian brain sends information that triggers the hypothalamus in the limbic system. The limbic system signals the cortex to be more alert and conscious.

The limbic system also works with the reptilian brain to keep the fight-or-flight reaction in homeostasis. This prevents stress from becoming chronic. The amygdala in the limbic system acts as the survival trigger, which detects danger and reacts with fear to any external threat. For future reference, it also stores such past experiences as emotionally dangerous or significant. When the amygdala detects a similar threat, it alerts the limbic system, the reptilian system, and the prefrontal cortex to make them aware of the dangerous situation. These systems interact and get involved to extinguish the fearful reactions.

The Brain in Synchrony

When I had CFIDS, my hormone system was totally out of whack. My emotional life was erratic, as I overreacted to everything and everyone. As I recovered from this illness, my brain structure connections were brought back into balance and proper communication was restored. I was fortunate to have found the tools to quiet my mind and reduce the reactivity of my emotions that had contributed to the imbalance. Meditation was my answer to keeping the communication doors opened. The prefrontal cortex regulates our emotional reactions and is the part of the brain that decides to turn off the fear switch. In my case, because of my emotional imbalance, the direct connection between the amygdala (the so-called fear gland) and the prefrontal cortex was not being made. It wasn't until I became conscious and used mind training that the Flow reconnected them. I would know that the connection was made when the anxiety stopped, my body became relaxed, and my mind could focus. I was no longer in a fog, unable to function.

An imbalance can easily occur in our everyday life to shut down the inner Flow. For example, one day I had expectations about how I wanted my day to proceed, but things didn't work out and my reaction wasn't helpful. I was to meet someone for lunch, and they never showed up or called to let me know they couldn't make it. I waited, called the person on my cell phone, became hopeful when someone came to the door, and was depressed when it wasn't my lunch date. I was angry that my time was wasted and at the same time felt guilty thinking maybe it was the wrong day. My mind went on and on with this broken stream of thoughts and feelings.

Looking back at my negative reaction to the situation, I see how it activated the sympathetic programs of the autonomic nervous system. I felt my stomach tense and noticed the clenching and unclenching of my hands and jaw. This caused my heart rate to increase, the blood vessels to constrict, and my blood pressure to rise. My emotional response ranged from irritation to rejection, then to sadness, anger, and hurt. At one point I realized what was occurring, that I had a choice about my thinking and emotional reactions. I switched my attention from the missed luncheon date to notice what I was feeling and thinking about the situation. As I became aware of my feelings, the amygdala calmed down and messages were sent to the prefrontal cortex to stop the fear syndrome. Without this awareness, the emotional buildup would have overridden the cortex and totally inhibited the process of bringing me back into balance.

The limbic system has an impact on the cortex and its rational functioning. The reptilian brain stimulates the cortex, when then interacts with the limbic system. The cortex receives external world information from the reptilian brain. It actively interprets this, synthesizes the information in order to decide whether (as in the case of my luncheon situation) the expectations match or conflict with perceived reality. This matching process leads to specific emotional responses dictating behavior. So, while I was waiting for my luncheon date, my reptilian brain took in all the external sensations, got the information to the limbic brain, where it was evaluated against previous experiences, and I went through my emotional response. If I had not consciously interrupted this emotional reaction, the memory would have been stored in my limbic system and would elicit an automatic response at a similar future event, keeping the whole pattern locked out of conscious awareness. This would likely affect my behavior regarding calling the person about missing the luncheon or whether I ever asked that person out to lunch again. In this example, the triggered inner response of hurt and anger was being stored until I interrupted it consciously.

From this story, you can begin to understand that the regulatory factors of the cortex play an important role in the management of emotional behavior. It doesn't mean that we are always consciously aware of our emotions, especially when we become angry or feel threatened by someone's remarks or actions. Our logic may tell us there is nothing to be concerned about, while our internal responses tell us differently. There can then be a large discrepancy between our thinking mind, our emotions, and our actual behavior.

I had a client who was told by her father when she was growing up that she should never wear tight-fitting clothes because she didn't have a good figure. This woman has a very nice figure and knows it, but she still continued to wear loose-fitting clothing. As we worked on this unconscious controlling issue, she became aware of this discrepancy by investigating her repressed memory, which very naturally shifted her emotions and belief about her body. I was later delighted when I saw her at an event in tight jeans. The pathways from the reptilian through the limbic to the cortex were in balance for her once again.

One final thought about the limbic system is that it seems to be responsible for triggering the sometimes strange phenomena of altered states of consciousness that some people experience. This can involve such phenomena as loss of body boundaries, feelings of floating or flying, and strange visual experiences of white light and even encountering nonhuman entities. Of course, deep meditation is also an altered state of consciousness.

Cortex Connections

Continuing to examine the interrelations of the four brain regions, we move to the top of the brain stem where the thalamus is centrally located in the cerebrum. This is the sensation-processing center of the cerebral cortex. It is a complex, highly organized relay station. This center is primarily governed by alpha brain waves and the neurotransmitter acetylcholine. Many of the sensory signals received by the central nervous system are relayed through the thalamus, which connects to various parts of the brain via the RAS. The thalamus relays information to all areas of the cortex and the limbic system. It passes on only those impulses that require immediate attention. It sorts out stimuli so our brains do not become overloaded. The thalamus also receives emotional information from the limbic system that contributes to our nonverbal facial expressions, creative thinking, and imagination.

Without the thalamus and the alpha waves, we would not know what it is to be calm and know that we are actually in our body or that we even have a body. When we are aware of the sensations the thalamus processes, they make us realize that we are solid and in this three-dimensional reality. The thalamus grounds us from overstimulated emotions or becoming too lost in our thinking mind. When the thalamus communication system gets disrupted and the Flow is interrupted, conditions such as Parkinson's disease, epilepsy, and bipolar disorder may occur.

The cerebral cortex connects to all the levels and regions of brain, as described previously. It receives and organizes all the incoming messages from the thalamus. It cognitively regulates the data of previously stored memories, and it can foresee the future consequences of actions by this memory comparison; it then connects to the limbic system to send out appropriate hormones into the biochemical structure of the body. It sends motor commands to the various muscles of the body, and it changes the neural activation of brain structures. Cognitive processes in the cortex can also be connected to the RAS, which maintains an alert and awakened mind, noting the arising of automatic patterns. The connection between the cortex and the RAS makes distorted thinking less likely.

There is a close interplay among abstract thoughts of a conscious cortex, the subconscious memories of the limbic brain, and the unconscious reactions of the reptilian brain. Your entire brain mobilizes, for instance, the stress (fight-or-flight) reaction. It can happen in response to a situation like being late for an appointment when the reaction is triggered by both conscious and unconscious thoughts. Alternatively, you might explain a complex idea to another person by first forming it in your mind, finding words to express it, using your speech apparatus, making facial expressions and using illustrative hand gestures, observing the other person's reactions for cues on how well you're communicating the idea, and experiencing the emotional tone of the whole situation. Thinking is really a whole-brain function, indeed a whole-body function.

The prefrontal brain is our CEO connected to every level of our brain. Long-term memories are not stored at specific synapses but are distributed throughout the whole-brain network of interconnecting neural pathways in such a way that any part of the network contains the basic pattern of the memory, while the whole network reproduces the personality structure. By the patterns of rhythmic electrical activity of the brain consolidated by chemical changes, we have the experience of who we are and become identified with this pattern. It becomes permanently encoded throughout the brain network, which holds positive and negative identity patterns. Most of this I-me-mine identity is below conscious awareness.

Our personality, our identity, is located in our prefrontal lobe. This was discovered in the 1800s in the famous case of a man by the name of Phineas Gage, a railroad worker. Gage had an almost fatal accident when a steel bar was plunged through the neocortex in the front part of his head. His frontal lobe was damaged and altered by the accident. When the bar was removed, he seemed normal, with no apparent physical disabilities from the accident. He survived, but it took a toll on his life. It was soon revealed that his personality had changed. Before the accident, Gage was a gentle, loving, and kind person. After the accident, he was a moody, negative, and difficult person who couldn't hold a job. It became clear to his doctors that the frontal lobe of the brain had something to do with his mental perception and positive states of mind.

This is a pivotal incident in brain research as it shows where personality is housed. Damage to the frontal region by stroke, advanced alcoholism, or heavy drug use affects the personality. It also diminishes the capacity for abstract thought, conception of a future action, formulation of an intention, carrying out a logical sequence of actions, or making judgments. The case of Phineas Gage is how we know that the frontal lobe acts as the CEO and orchestrates all other parts of the body, as well as identity and personality.

As discussed earlier, the prefrontal lobe is the newest addition to the brain and the most revolutionary in its functions. It offers the greatest opportunity for evolutionary change in that it allows the mind to evolve the brain consciously. Through the ages, people have created tools to help themselves evolve and become "awake, enlightened, or realized." The concept rather than the words used to describe it is what is important. The words do, however, indicate integration of all parts of the brain and a synchrony of electrical-chemical interactions that increases awareness and allows the individual to be fully in the present moment without a flood of thoughts clouding a direct perception of reality. The seekers discovered techniques and methods that took them into deep states of inner silence. As they evolved their brain-mind, their natural state became one of compassion, kindness, service, laughter, creativity, and deep connection to all living things.

Techniques and methods are tools to explore what only each of us can discover and claim for ourselves. I have rediscovered through years of practice and study some mind tools for our collective evolutionary journey. These tools are predominately orchestrated from the prefrontal lobe of the cortex. That is, they seem logical, rational, and available for any of us to understand, use, and practice. As we apply these tools, magic happens: Our minds become more conscious, clear, calm, and vibrant; we feel more relaxed; and our bodies move naturally back into balance. Their continued use will strengthen our minds until that mysterious aspect of our consciousness takes over and the magic of healing, peace, and joy emerges in our lives.

4

Training the Mind

"Training" the mind does not in any way mean forcibly subjugating or brainwashing the mind. To train the mind is first to see directly and concretely how the mind functions, a knowledge that you derive from spiritual teaching and through personal meditation practice. Then you use the understanding to tame the mind and work with it skillfully, to make it more and more pliable, so that you can become master of your mind and employ it to its fullest and most beneficial end.

—Sogyal Rinpoche

As I look back fondly on my first rigorous three-month silent meditation retreat, I see both the sweet and the ugly. I was one of a hundred men and women of all ages who came from around the world, eager to shift our consciousness. Together we started our day at 4 a.m. and finished at 9 p.m. Our daily schedule consisted of alternating an hour of sitting meditation with an hour of walking meditation. Meals were for an hour or two, with evening dharma talk for another hour and a meeting with a teacher for ten minutes every other day. The staff held us like caring parents in a safety net looking after our needs with focused attention.

I thrived in this environment of consistency and repetition; I found that it supported and created perseverance and endurance in me. I began to link each moment together like a long string of prayer beads. The repetition of repeat, repeat, and repeat brought my mind into a calm, clear, loving state—a trained state that permitted me to experience nature in a different way.

I took walks in the forest at lunchtime. The birds must have felt safe with my slow, quiet state because they became friendly and curious. Often they would fly down to perch on my hand or hang on my scarf. I would bring birdseed and marvel as they ate out of my hand, totally unafraid. It felt like I was Saint Francis with twenty birds all over my head, shoulders, and arms, chirping and fluttering about me.

One day I walked deeper into the forest and saw three deer grazing several yards ahead of me. I stood watching them for a long time. They would graze and then all three would suddenly lift their heads and look straight at me. Then they would graze a little more and then take a few steps toward where I was standing. Finally, there was a moment when the three deer lifted their heads and walked slowly toward me and I began to walk toward them. We edged slowly closer and closer until something changed that magic moment of interspecies relationship. My mind shifted. I literally saw and felt fear moving through me. If I put thoughts to that moment, it would be, "Will they hurt me?" Just as gently as the deer were moving toward me, they gently turned and headed the other way. It was my fear that separated us from that magic moment of connection and relationship.

For the rest of the retreat, I focused on the mental tools that would let me reduce my fear and open to new and unexpected experiences. Having mental tools trains the mind to be consistent with positive emotions that can keep us in balance and harmony in any situation we face, but to integrate these tools into our lives takes practice. Let me say it again. It takes practice. It is the consistency of practice in training the mind that will change our lives.

The Four Mental Tools

The knowledge of brain-wave patterns gave me a context that clarified my years of meditation practice. This knowledge has taken the mystique out of meditation and has given me a picture of how my mind functions when I am in the various states of awareness. I now know that I have a choice about what goes through my mind and that I can train my mind. One of the Buddha's comments about training the mind has stuck with me over the years. He described the dilemma of meditation in the following way:

> In days gone by, this mind of mine used to stray wherever selfish desire or lust or pleasure would lead it. Today the mind does not stray. It sits under the harmony of control, even as a wild elephant is trained.

The Buddha describes the internal conflict we have as we begin to train our minds. His metaphor is that it is as hard as training a wild elephant. From my own experience and observing those I teach, I see that the conflict arises from our reason, determination, desires, and attachments. With our reason, we rationalize that we already know how to do it. With our determination, we start but don't sustain the practice that can actually change brain functions. We all know how our desires and attachments can distract us. Passing pleasures entice us and old patterns of dullness and passivity make it hard to summon the sustained discipline needed to meditate regularly. Such conflicts arise in all of us when we are challenged to train the mind.

Remember, these conflicts are physiological as well as psychological. They are deep-seated patterns that arose from the brain's electrical-chemical interactions over long periods of time. For example, I know that after dinner my desire for dessert is often stronger than my mental intent to abstain from eating sugar, which I also know is not good for me. Yet my desire often overrides my intent to stay healthy. Why is this? This conflict comes from a misalignment between the reasoning function of the neocortex and the emotional desires of the limbic system, which can inhibit my commitment to reduce sugar intake. In mind training this same predicament exists. "Should I meditate or watch that new movie on DVD?" I constantly hear people say that they just don't have time to meditate.

You will face these inner conflicts, so I provide some mind principles and instructions on how to bring your mental intent and emotional resistance into alignment. But you still have the basic challenge of using the tools and engaging in the daily practice. Will you meet this challenge? Stop reading, close your eyes, and feel your body. Is it telling you, "Yes, it is time to deepen my life"? Or is it saying, "Read on, but don't pressure yourself. There will be another opportunity to embrace this journey. Be caring and patient with yourself"? Each of us has a unique and perfectly timed journey. Trust yourself. Listen to yourself.

Each step in our lives depends on our intention and where we choose to put our attention. Intention and attention are the foundations of mind training, along with receptivity and awareness. These four tools are what we use to create the alignment and produce the changes we want in our lives. We will use these four mental tools in each of the four brain-wave meditation processes. These mind tools or functions are located primarily in the prefrontal lobe, the CEO of our brain. So with the CEO's guidance, we will use them to train and awaken our mind. I will now describe each of these four mind tools. Notice which one of them you are most conscious of either needing or using in your life at this time.

Intention is the first mental tool. To have intention is to have a purpose, or a direction. Your brain likes direction, and in each brain meditation it will need a different intention due to the specific way that part of the brain functions. When you give yourself intentional directions, you give each level of your brain a specific focus to explore how that brain-mind functions. For example, you will set your intention to relax, or to be aware of your sensations, or to have emotional awareness, or to expand beyond the boundaries of your body into space. Each pattern is purposeful to what will arise in your field of awareness. *Intention is about "what."*

Attention is the second mental tool, and it is where you place your focus. Attention and intention together are the glue that holds each moment as it moves into the next moment. Osho, an Indian philosopher, said, "Existence wants you to be so intelligent, smart, and quick that it gives you only one moment at a time." Intentions link these moments with your actions, and with focus they establish a field of awareness. This field would not exist unless you had the focused attention to understand, grasp, appreciate, recognize, and cognize.

Attention is the central core to experiencing the mind. Whatever your intention, for example, observing your breath, you will notice with continual practice that the repeated aiming and focusing of attention sustain your intention. As the flow of energy enters your conscious awareness, it regulates the energy of your mind in a new way. When the mind is sustained in a single-focused manner, it brings both balance and stability. This is what is meant by concentration. Since attention is pivotal to how we focus the mind, it is the essential tool used to reduce stress. *Attention is about "where."*

Receptivity is the third tool. It allows you to perceive what is in your mind. When you do not resist and just accept what is in the mind, whether it is pain, fast-moving thoughts, deep feelings, or just space, this receptivity brings centeredness and strength to your life. Without this ability to be self-observant and receptive, we seem to lose awareness of our thought stream, and then we seem to lose control of our minds. This can lead to feelings of going crazy. Learning to be receptive to your brain-mind activity, whether it is positive or negative, will eventually bring you to the essence of your being. Being open-minded and knowing how to turn inward enable your mind to become more sensitive to inner changes, more responsive to your own needs, more flexible to confront challenges, and more willing to confront your own mental, emotional, and physical resistances. Being receptive to what is occurring right now, right here, disrupts past thoughts and automatic influences. Receptivity is the essence of the moment. When you are truly receptive, the world will change in you and around you naturally. *Receptivity is about "when."*

Awareness is the fourth tool. It is what you use to observe yourself and others. Awareness comes from being attentive and is used to make the distinction between your inner and outer experience of life. It is easy to get lost in the randomness of your thoughts. Intention, attention, and receptivity stop you from being carried away by mental activity. Awareness is "tuned in" to purposeful observing and open to whatever is occurring in the moment. Inner awareness is the ability to look calmly at yourself without judgment and without intervention. Awareness notices your thoughts and emotions as they arise, like watching passing clouds linked to a much larger dimensional background of space. With this kind of awareness, you have a sense of curiosity about what is happening in the moment. Awareness opens you to meaning, purpose, hope, and the experience of how to expand your life. It helps you gain access to the workings of the automatic ego personality, penetrating the thick veil of the self-centered "me, my, and mine" activity of your mind. Awareness is the laser that pierces your unconscious patterns and memories to see the "truth" of what you have been hiding from yourself. Once you know how that resistance came about, the reaction ceases to develop. *Awareness is about "how."*

Your intention reflects the quality of mind you want. Where to place your attention is a choice. I notice that what I place my attention on is directly related to the quality of mind I want to experience, and this has changed my meditation practice. It has also changed it for the many people I teach. One of the people in my meditation circle commented that for years she had meditated with music and with guided meditation tapes. After all these years of meditation, she realized her attention had been unfocused, and she didn't know where to place her intention with attention. She didn't know how to use her awareness as a tool to guide her to those places of mind that were opening in her. She told me that having the four brain-wave states as a context and knowing how to use these mental tools, she was able to go deeper inside herself and open the locked doors of her mind. More important, she felt grounded, present, happy, and was moving into a more creative expression in her life. And she was able to generate more beta brain activity from the meditation, which created a clearer, quicker mind to think, act, and solve problems in her life.

She wrote to me about her experience using the Mind Tools: "For years in meditation, I thought it was ok to 'zone out' or as I put it 'be taken out by Spirit' in the middle of meditation. I felt I was getting all that I needed even if I wasn't present while meditating. Though that may be true, I have found, through Patt's meditation teachings, that staying present is what allows me to now go very deep into my meditation and remember the benefit of it all."

Another Tool: The Enneagram

To utilize the four mental tools properly, you need to understand how your ego or personality type approaches mind training. What I have found most useful in understanding the patterns of my personality is the Enneagram. It is a personality typology that shows us what we become fixated on and therefore our resistance to life's flow. It points to the patterns that make us both happy and unhappy. It teaches us what generates our patterns of stress and what conditions we need to create, to integrate, and to grow in our lives. The interesting paradox of the Enneagram is that it shows us how our personality-ego structure is *who we are not.* That is, it reveals the compensatory patterns we developed from our family conditioning and onward throughout life; it also shows the innate genetic patterns that create our strengths and weaknesses.

Personality is a function of how the brain-mind interacts and responds. The Enneagram is extremely useful for understanding the personality system, which is actually a set of conditioned experiences working together as parts of a mechanism. Once you are aware of your Enneagram type, it will aid in training your mind, as well as opening new insights into the resistant patterns that arise in meditation. Through the lens of the Enneagram, you will see how your personality is encoded in every part of your body and brain, and see the implications of your reactions, habits, and automatic thoughts. You will face the difficult truth that your personality is a mechanized system, but that you can free it of its conditioned rigidity. As you learn to work with personality in your mind training, many of the physical, emotional, and mental patterns you have lived with for years can be changed through the conscious development of your brain and mind.

In my own personal development over the years, I've worked with the Jungian-oriented typology of personality as well as other systems. The Enneagram has been for me the most useful personality typology for mind training. After working with it for a few years, my personality, or who I think I am, is much less of a mystery and I now see it much more objectively. From the Buddhist perspective, personality is no more than an accumulation of our sensations, emotions, thoughts, perceptions, and beliefs. But when you are immersed in these traits, it is difficult to sort them out and make distinctions. In training the mind to observe its own distractions and dysfunctions, it is imperative to know and understand your personality structure. The Enneagram system provides you with that tool. Looking through this lens to explore your habitual ego traits is a way to increase self-inquiry, release self-defeating patterns, and allow for change and growth.

The Enneagram

We are each a dominant type...

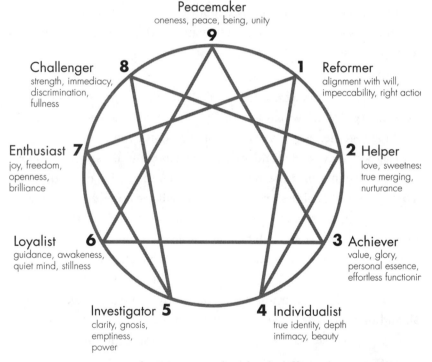

Peacemaker
oneness, peace, being, unity
9

Challenger **8**
strength, immediacy,
discrimination,
fullness

1 Reformer
alignment with will,
impeccability, right action

Enthusiast **7**
joy, freedom,
openness,
brilliance

2 Helper
love, sweetness
true merging,
nurturance

Loyalist **6**
guidance, awakeness,
quiet mind, stillness

3 Achiever
value, glory,
personal essence,
effortless functioning

Investigator **5**
clarity, gnosis,
emptiness,
power

4 Individualist
true identity, depth
intimacy, beauty

...yet there are individual differences

Adapted from Riso and Hudson

Psychology is focused on the hows and whys of behavior, thought processes, emotions, motivations, relationships, potentials, and pathologies. The Enneagram performs the same function, and helps people overcome or better manage pathologies as well as transcend perceived limitations. It is a system that describes nine personality types; each has a definite profile of how that type relates to itself, to others, and to the social environment, and each has specific directions to guide that type to psychological health and spiritual liberation. During the past two decades, the Enneagram has undergone a renewal of interest in the Western world. This personality development system is arguably one of the oldest on the planet.

History of the Enneagram

The word *enneagram* means "a nine-pointed graphic symbol." This symbol shows how the nature of personality structure impacts every part of life. In the symbol, each of its nine points is a distinct personality denoting one type. The Enneagram symbol is made up of two parts: a triangle, and a seven-point configuration that overlays the triangle. This symbol has been found as far back as ten thousand years ago in pre-Egyptian temples. What we know about the history of the Enneagram is that it has been used in esoteric spiritual communities for thousands of years to guide seekers to develop themselves. The current Enneagram has its roots in Middle Eastern traditions and was taught in certain schools of Islamic Sufism. It first appeared in the West through the teachings of the Russian mystic, G. I. Gurdjieff. In 1968, Oscar Ichazo, a Bolivian student of esoteric teachings, founded the Arica School with its modern interpretation of the Enneagram of Personality, identifying nine personality types and how each becomes fixed in the psyche at an early stage of development.

Several people from the Arica School began teaching the Enneagram in the United States and then around the world. In the past thirty years, its use has spread into religious, educational, and even business communities as a way not only to understand personality structure, but also how to develop oneself by understanding personality patterns.

As the brain-mind evolves and becomes more conscious, it must become aware of the self as its personality. Psychologists have confirmed that personality development is highly influenced by parents or significant others early in life. We can see for ourselves that heredity factors establish a child's temperament and attitudes. The Enneagram type represents the way the child has adapted to the parents' way of life and their environment and culture. Enneagram typology includes both the genetics as well as the conditions in which the child is raised.

Understanding the dynamics of your type provides the key elements of your thought patterns. When you are developing new brain-mind practices, you will be able to more readily identify your blocks and resistances. You will also become less engaged in issues about protecting your personality. In the process of increasing brain-mind potential, attachment to personality issues takes up a great amount of attention and energy that could otherwise be used to further the process. Gaining understanding of your Enneagram type will provide clearer understanding of those issues. As with any unconscious quality, once the pattern of your personality is revealed and acknowledged by you, it becomes quiet and has less power over you.

The points of clarification I list here about the Enneagram are to give you a context for how understanding your personality type is essential for the development of mind training in meditation. There are many books and training programs on the Enneagram, and I encourage you to take the time to study and learn in depth about who you are as a personality. The long history of the Enneagram shows that it has always been used as a psychospiritual tool to aid in the larger quest for personal liberation, enlightenment, and awakening. I likewise value it and use it in this context.

Here are a few essential clarifications about the Enneagram:

1. Your Enneagram type does not change over time. Each unique personality type remains the same until the end of your life. It is your level of health, development, and growth that changes.

2. The Enneagram type is used for men as well as women as it is a universal typology. Children can also be typed at an early age, and there are many new books on this particular subject.

3. Each of the nine types has a range of psychological states that move from a healthy to an unhealthy state of expression. These different states are encompassed within each type.

4. Your Enneagram type description will hold less emotional charge for you as you understand and learn how to work with it. As you recognize your positive and negative personality traits, you will become more objective, less attached to them, and healthier.

5. Each type is no better than another. There is no hierarchy in this system. For example, personality type one is not better than nine. Each type has its weaknesses and its strengths. As you will see, every person has characteristics from all the types, but one is pointedly, more distinctly you. The ability to understand your own type and those of family members, friends, and others in the larger community reduces judgment, increases compassion, and opens the doors for deeper and more profound relationships with others.

Personality Typing

For a time I was a student in religious studies at Marylhurst University in Portland, Oregon. Our first assignment was to take an Enneagram assessment. The sister who taught the class was insistent that to further our studies it would be beneficial to know our personality type. After taking the assessment, I had three types with similarly high scores. Many of us had multiples, and we were told to study each of those types to see which one fit best. Two of them had some personality aspects with which I could identify, but one fit absolutely perfectly. I recognized "me" in personality type six. One of the general labels given to type six is the Loyalist. The description of all the coping skills, childhood patterns, and how I was attached to the world was a complete match for me. Don Riso and Russ Hudson, founders of the Enneagram Institute in Stone Ridge, New York, and authors of numerous books on the Enneagram, describe six as: "The Committed, Security-Oriented Type: Engaging, Responsible, Anxious, and Suspicious."

As I explored the many aspects of the Enneagram system about my type, I was amazed and struck by the ingenious nature of the Enneagram design and how it could nail me so accurately. Beyond intellectual understanding, it gave me handles for how my patterns and reactions impacted my thought process, increased my stress, and challenged my relationships. This self-identification system provides a constant mirror and an honest appraisal of where I am at any moment in my life. This appraisal has led me to deep self-inquiry and acceptance of my foibles, as well as instilled confidence in my strengths and gifts. Working with the Enneagram has released chronic tension from striving to do or have things, or be someone that is not part of my energetic system. Most important, I am grateful for the capabilities of others and appreciative of my own.

The description of each Enneagram type provides an indispensable framework for self-knowledge and personal growth. Before I give brief descriptions of each of the nine types, describe yourself. Most of us begin with physical characteristics, our roles in the world (marital status, employment, etc.), interests, and hobbies. We may also include our talents, beliefs, humor quotient, our sensitivity, whether introverted or extraverted, and our ambitions and striving. These last personality qualities are habitual and are the basis of our automatic thoughts that have become fixed patterns.

The Enneagram shows us our mental habits in a very clear mirror. These automatic patterns also resonate with the reptilian brain's capability of selective attention, which can selectively limit what it hears, experiences, and expresses. This selective attention pattern operates twofold in our conscious habitual expression. Take as an example a belief pattern that you hold. It unconsciously informs how you respond to and in the world. If another belief that does not match this belief comes into your consciousness, you often dismiss it through selective attention. José Ortega y Gasset says, "Tell me to what you pay attention and I will tell you who you are."

One example is my belief that the world is unsafe and I must protect myself. This theme unconsciously crops up when I least expect it. For instance, when I lose something, I immediately have the thought,

"Someone has taken it." Since I am not safe in the world, I can't trust others. And so it goes.

Much of our selected attention has been developed by our early childhood conditioning. Each Enneagram type reflects early childhood messages that our parents unintentionally ingrained in us. To cope with our childhood situation, we developed strategies to survive. We learned how to use our innate talents and abilities to feel safe and to deal with the situation into which we were born. As a result of the continual reinforcement of these childhood messages, we formed an early sense of self. Our personality began to fit like a glove, its survival patterns adapted to fit our environment.

It constantly amazes me how millions of people in each personality type have developed similar coping strategies. As you use the Enneagram as a dynamic feedback tool, it will reveal that your personality is just a set of conditioned patterns. It is not who you really are. Remember this "me" identity we call the self is a construct and is primarily located in the neocortex of the brain. As we have seen, if any damage occurs in the prefrontal lobe, the personality will change. The personality is as plastic as the brain and is conditioned by and can change your automatic patterns. The Enneagram can be used to break through the structure of your personality-ego to help you make choices as they arise in your practice, mind training, and meditation.

To know your personality type speeds up the reprogramming of the unconscious awareness that I describe as a "sleep state." I have found that the Enneagram helps us get out of our "negative feedback loops" that so easily trap us. From that breakthrough, it can point us in the direction of positive growth and maturity. Below is a one-line description of each of the nine personality types. The Enneagram system is much more sophisticated and richer in depth than just these one-line descriptions, but it will give you a starting point.

Based on these one-line descriptions, which type do you think you are?

1. **One** is the reformer who wants to fix the world and make it a perfect place to live.

2. **Two** is the caregiver who cares for everyone in order to get the love he/she wants.

3. **Three** is an achiever, a productive leader who works efficiently to receive the recognition he/she needs.

4. **Four** is a very unique person, an individualist who is highly creative but feels he/she is not enough.

5. **Five** is one who investigates deeply into the details of things and personally and emotionally separates from life.

6. **Six** is loyal, kind, and needs security and direction to feel safe and secure in an unsafe world.

7. **Seven** is the adventurer, always active to find happy experiences, and avoids feeling pain.

8. **Eight** is the challenger with a forceful personality who stands strong for justice and for the good of all.

9. **Nine** is the peacemaker who will backpedal and avoid conflict in his/her life so that peace will prevail.

In *The Wisdom of the Enneagram,* Riso and Hudson assert: "Our personality is an important part of our development. It is necessary for the refinement of our essential nature. The problem is that we get stuck in the personality and don't know how to move to the next phase." In mind training, you will use the Enneagram types as a way to become aware of your mind and also to experience your essential nature. It is a meditative tool for change.

What's Your Enneagram Type?

To find out what Enneagram type you are, I recommend consulting one of the books on the subject listed in the bibliography or visiting the website of the Enneagram Institute for a free Enneagram assessment (http://www.enneagraminstitute.com/Tests_Battery.asp).

After you have identified your type, summarize for yourself the elements that make up your type, such as your gifts, when you are at your best and worst, your general behaviors, and what your impact is on others. In my case, my gifts as a type six are that I am determined, trustworthy, and cooperative. I am at my best and healthy when I feel secure. I am courageous and decisive. In my average mode, I am dutiful, I worry over everything, and I am prepared and organized. Others feel I am fully engaged with them, and they don't feel excluded when I am with them. I am so interested in others that they can feel I am cross-examining them. When I am in an unhealthy mode, I am paranoid, panicky, unreliable, and self-punishing.

You can use your Enneagram type characteristics to observe the elements of your personality pattern. When you are doing certain mind-training practices, elements of your type pattern will begin to produce, on the one hand, resistance, fear, anxiety, uncertainty, guilt, and confusion; and on the other hand, you will be able to access strength, determination, concentration, kindness, and willpower, among other positive characteristics. I had a client who refused to see herself as an enneagram type four. She did not want to acknowledge and totally resisted the fact that she could be temperamental, moody, and self-pitying. After some discussion, she saw that these qualities were the result of not accepting her writing talent and ability to create beauty in her life.

Besides easily recognizable behavioral characteristics, the Enneagram also identifies the emotional traits of your personality, which are stored in the subconscious mind of the limbic system. Therefore, you may have a hard time accepting some of your emotional characteristic because you are unconscious of them. Some of these unconscious traits are your core beliefs, the emotions that run you, your sense of self, your inner childhood messages, and your coping strategies.

A client who is a type one on the enneagram was at a social gathering. He was having a discussion with a group of people and there was a difference of opinion. To convince the group he was right, he raised his voice louder and louder until he dominated the conversation. Type one copes with this kind of situation by bulldozing. As a child, the type one received the message that he must be right, in fact, it was not OK to make mistakes. Until type ones look at these blind spots of behavioral responses and reactions, they will continue to create stress in their lives.

The conscious-subconscious dynamic reminds me of a lake where we see birds landing on the water, the ripples from a branch dropping, waves rolling into the shore, boats drifting, and plants floating on the surface of the lake. We observe all of this activity but are unaware of what is going on beneath the surface of the water. The subconscious qualities of your personality are beneath the surface. Until you place your attention on them, you are not fully aware of them.

The Enneagram reveals these subconscious traits. As you move your conscious attention beneath the surface into your subconscious mind, it becomes possible to perceive what you have been unknowingly and habitually expressing in your everyday life. The limbic subconscious part of your mind acts like your shadow. Your shadow slides into consciousness what you feel ashamed of or have rejected or repressed. You, like all of us, spontaneously and unknowingly project your shadow onto others. We all have patterns we are aware of and ones of which we are unaware. You will know the shadow is speaking and projecting its contents when you have compulsive reactions and say negative things about someone or something. You can ignore your response or become conscious of it and learn to embrace this denied aspect. You do have a choice. When you learn to be conscious of these personality patterns, they no longer have power over you. They no longer hold you in their unconscious grip. When that happens, you begin to experience true inner freedom and happiness grows naturally within you. Carl Jung says, "That which we don't bring to consciousness is experienced as fate." And fate, as we know, means the gods don't give us a choice about our lives.

As a type six, the characteristic trait that continually hooks me is my self-doubt. For years, I was unconscious about its dysfunction in my life. It wasn't until I went deep into my subconscious mind at a meditation retreat that I found a childhood message telling me, "It's not OK to trust myself." I realized that I had been operating from the belief that I could only trust others, such as one of my parents, and could not trust myself. From a little girl onward, I focused my attention totally on the outside world to tell me that I was OK. Discovering this deep belief was a revelation. I realized how it had limited me in finding peace of mind from an inner authority and having a true sense of an inner home base. I was also surprised to realize how fearful I was, that this fear is my basic emotion. From my work with the Enneagram, I knew that the emotional source of a type six is fear. I didn't realize the extent of my anxiety, however. Until that meditation, I did not realize how addicted I had become to anxious feelings. Those feelings were my home, however unhappy they made me. Today my awareness is very selective. When I feel anxious, I investigate it, embrace the feeling, and then consciously shift my attention to that place down inside of me that I call my home base. This keeps stress and tension in constant check. Awareness, attention, receptivity, and intention are the keys to unlocking dysfunctional personality stress for me.

I give this example from my own experience to illustrate how practice with mind tools can heal long forgotten dysfunctional patterns in your life. As you continue to heal yourself consciously and unconsciously, your brain, body, and mind change; they grow and evolve to transform you into a more integrated and whole human being.

In part II, as you work with the mind tools in each of the four brain-wave patterns, you will integrate the Enneagram work with the mind-training principles and meditation practices.

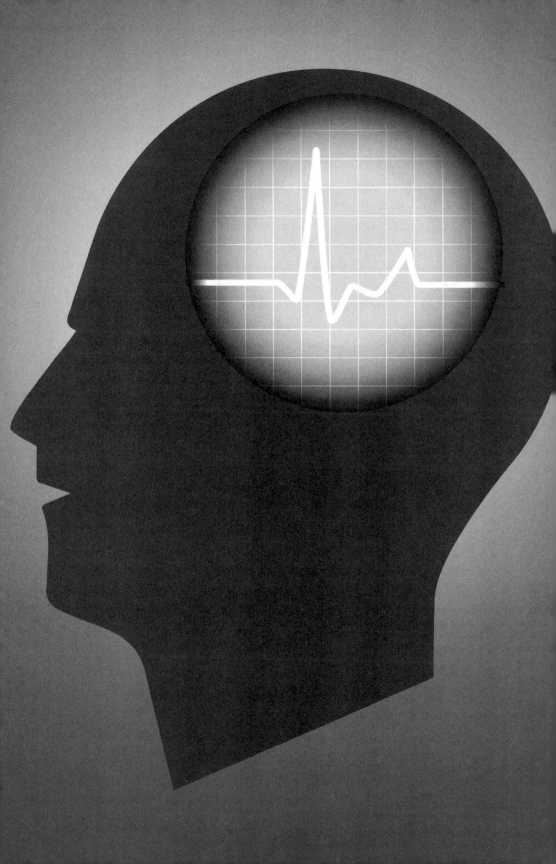

PART II

MEDITATION AS MIND
TECHNOLOGY

Introduction

The earliest record of meditation techniques is found in the Hindu Vedic scriptures written in 1500 BCE. With Gautama the Buddha around 500 BCE, there was a significant dissemination of meditation practices across the Asian continent, with each culture adapting it into their religious and spiritual practice. As Islam spread throughout the Middle East, Africa, and then into Asia in the twelfth century, the Sufis, a mystical sect of Islam, brought their practice of meditation. Through reflection on love and mystical poetry, they found that they could gather their scattered thoughts and become present in the experience of their life. The discovery of a figure of a yogi found in the Indus Valley demonstrates that yoga practice and meditation techniques could have existed in the first Indian civilization approximately 3300 BCE. As civilized societies began to emerge, meditation evolved into a structured practice or a technology.

Thousands of years after its widespread use in Asia, meditation became known in the Western world, particularly through Christian mystics and monks. Saint Ignatius of Loyola (1491–1556) wrote Contemplation to Attain Love to encourage monks to both visualize and intellectually contemplate Christ's life. Until the middle of the twentieth century, meditation was mostly practiced within religious sects. In the 1960s and '70s, meditation was popularized in the West through books and self-help television programs. The interest in meditation by such cultural icons as the Beatles spread its popularity, particularly among the Boomer generation.

One of the most popular meditation practices of this period was Transcendental Meditation (TM), which involved silently repeating a simple phrase or mantra over and over for twenty minutes at a time. This method was taught in workshops all across the United States. The claim was that TM would instill a centered calmness so people could perform more effectively in daily life. In the 1970s and '80s, a number of Americans went to India and Burma and brought back both Hindu and Buddhist techniques for personal meditation practice.

The Theravadan Buddhist practice of Vipassana or insight meditation gained a modest following, and it had an impact on the general public with its practice to reduce stress for both mental and physical well-being. Researchers such as Jon Kabat-Zinn, from the University of Massachusetts Medical School, wrote popular books on the value of meditation to cope with pain, stress, and anxiety. Using language from the Vipassana, he called his approach "mindfulness training."

From the 1990s to the present, there has been an increasing body of research on the positive affects of meditation practice. New meditation technologies and monitoring equipment have made meditation more acceptable to the psychology and medical fields, although the health benefits of meditation have long been recognized in the Eastern cultures where it originated. Meditation technologies have become a productive way of training the mind to reduce health problems and increase a person's potential and success in life. Stress reduction and relaxation programs have been instigated in hospital clinics to create greater levels of health and well-being for patients. Doctors now refer patients to meditation-based programs for medical problems such as headaches, high blood pressure, back pain, cancer, and heart disease. Some patients are taught to prepare for the stress of surgery with meditation techniques that relax them and keep their minds in a positive quiet state of calm that appears to accelerate healing after the surgery.

The mental tools and meditation practices you will find in the next four chapters, each devoted to one of the four brain-wave patterns (beta, alpha, theta, and delta), provide you access to all of the benefits of meditation and much more. You can enter the four brain-mind states in meditation, then return to normal living, and be fully enriched, enlivened, and mentally and emotionally enhanced. As a result of practicing meditation, you will feel more alive, more creative, more peaceful, steadier, and calmer. It leads to a deeper level of physical relaxation and more understanding and insights about others and yourself. You will also be less likely to be rattled, experience being kinder to others and more open to situations, and respond to difficulties with greater ease. In addition, through these practices, you will reprogram and evolve your brain to a higher state of consciousness and function.

The Benefits of Meditation

Physiological Benefits	Mental/Spiritual Benefits
Leads to a deeper level of physical relaxation	Reduces emotional distress
Lowers high blood pressure due to less stimulation of the autonomic and central nervous systems	Leads to a more balanced and present state of mind
Increases blood flow and slows the heart rate	Improves focus, attention, and concentration
Reduces fear and anxiety by lowering blood lactate	Improves cognitive function, thus increases the ability to learn
Reduces pain and headaches by decreasing muscle tension	Increases creativity
Reduces viral activity	Increases ability to be calm, alert, and peaceful
Enhances the immune system by increasing the activity of natural killer cells, which kill bacteria and cancer cells	Increases awareness, insight, and intuition
Promotes deep breathing, which reduces the accumulation of carbon dioxide that causes acidosis and reduction of brain cells	Increases positive thinking, goodness, and compassion
Increases synchrony in neural circuitry, which produces positive changes in the structure and function of the brain	Increases ability to shift beyond ordinary consciousness
Stabilizes the nervous system, which reduces stress	Enhances self-mastery of busy thoughts
Enhances postoperative healing by reducing stress and improving immunity	Stabilizes emotional reactions
Increases serotonin production, which regulates mood and behavior associated with insomnia, depression, and obesity	Builds self-confidence and wisdom

Today, meditation training is out of the religious closet and has moved into our lives through many cultural avenues. Whether used to solve medical problems, increase optimal performance in athletes, help business executives make better decisions, or awaken you to who you really are, these ancient methods for venturing inward and finding your own answers to life's challenges are a counterbalance to a consumer-driven society that tells you that the answers are outside of you.

As a quick visual-kinesthetic review in preparation for the chapters that follow, return to the model of the brain structures using your closed hand, as described in part I. Recall that the neocortex is in your fingers and this is the origin of beta brain waves. The parietal lobe of the cortex is in your knuckles and that is where alpha waves occur. Your thumb underneath your fingers against the palm represents the limbic system and is the source of theta brain waves. The palm of your hand going down into your wrist is the reptilian brain where delta brain waves originate. We will now begin to explore each brain wave and brain structure separately, beginning with the beta brain waves and the neocortex.

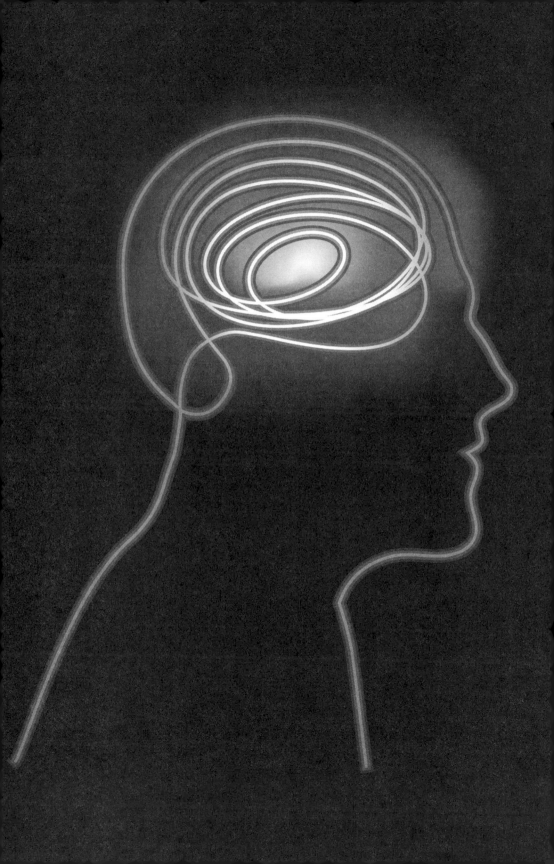

5

Beta Brain Waves and Dopamine

When an archer shoots for nothing, he has all his skill. If he shoots for a brass buckle, he is already nervous. If he shoots for a prize of gold, he goes blind. Or, if he sees two targets he is out of his mind! He thinks more of winning than of shooting, and the need to win drains him of power.

—Chuan Tzu, a Taoist sage

I n our fast-paced culture, we are often caught up in competition, a whirlwind of activity, multitasking as we feel the constant pressure to do more and do it faster. The problem, as Chuan Tzu suggests in the opening quote, is that the need to win, succeed, get the job done, and so on drains us of our real power. What drives our fast pace and feeds our addiction to success is our mental perspective, and the brain wave that supports and reinforces this particular perspective is the beta wave. Beta is our thinking brain wave. Its activity is fast and goal driven. It reflects our constant mental focus and the pace and speed of our activity as we work and play. If you were a car in beta, you would be topping out the rpm's in every gear.

Beta is your dominant brain-mind rhythm, and it reflects a mind state that is generally very alert and focused but can easily become agitated, unclear, and impatient. The power of thinking is well recognized, but not so the power of awareness. The use of beta brain waves in meditation is to redirect your awareness to your inner self and refocus your attention away from the outer world. You will find as you learn to refocus your inner awareness that you are not as physically, mentally, or emotionally drained, but instead will feel energized and less stressed out.

I am reminded of one of my Enneagram 3 clients. On afternoon, Sara, president of a consulting firm, barely made it to the airport to catch a flight. She felt stressed out and harried as she got to the gate. Then, as she walked down the aisle of the airplane to her seat, she spotted a woman she knew a few rows behind her. Sara was stunned because she had recently fired this woman and was in a bitter lawsuit with her for a million dollars. This put her stress level over the top and she wondered if she could handle the two-hour flight. As she buckled up, Sara remembered that she had my Beta Relaxation CD (see the appendix) on her iPod. She turned it on, put the earphones in her ears, and went into a peaceful mental state for two hours. She told me later that if it hadn't been for the relaxation meditation, she would have "lost it." Her stress response had become too intense to push down. At the end of the flight, she was calm and centered enough to be gracious to the woman as they disembarked from the plane. By choosing to be calm, Sara was also being gracious to herself as she placed her attention on reducing her high stress level.

Our constant inner jabbering of observations, judgments, rationalizations, assumptions, and plans is the beta-wave inner dialogue we have with ourselves that is hidden from other people. We would be embarrassed if our minds broadcasted aloud this stream of thoughts constantly going around in our heads. It seems there is no way to switch these thoughts off; they even keep going when we sleep. This mentally self-absorbed activity becomes our addiction. It is narrowly focused and compulsive, and blocks out the reality of what is actually happening around us. We are, in effect, holding a silent conversation with ourselves, rather than focusing on what is actually being presented to us from the outside. We meet a new person and it immediately brings to mind someone similar from our past, and we end up projecting our attitudes and judgments about that previous person onto this person in the present. Our preoccupation, indicated by high beta-wave activity, can keep us locked in a small world of our own making. If we can learn to retrain high beta-wave output to function in a different way, however, it can slow down this inner dialogue and actually expand our world and experience of reality.

This jabbering mind state is the realm of the newest part of human brain development. The fast beta brain waves are primarily produced in the neocortex with its neurotransmitter dopamine. The beta brain waves and dopamine are essential for sending cognitive information throughout the brain-mind as well as messages to the body. Beta regulates the circadian rhythms of the body such as sleep cycles, breathing, blood pressure, and sugar levels. Electrical beta waves send energy to the body in order to control metabolism, which is the ability of the body to break down, grow, reproduce, and maintain digestive structures. So when you are fretting over a mental concern, it affects the digestion of your food and the integrity of the digestive system.

A client with irritable bowel syndrome was able to alleviate the intense symptoms by using the relaxation techniques for reducing the high beta brain waves. Most of us know how to slow down our beta to affect our body. You have heard the term "just breathe" when faced with a difficult situation. If you become aware of your breath and slowly inhale and exhale, this action can slow the beta brain wave and the body gets the message to relax the muscle tightening in your stomach and reduce anxiety. We've all done this spontaneously to avoid stimulus overload of anxiety or fear.

My client Tom, an Enneagram 3, wrote a short note to me after we had worked together for several months. He wrote that if anyone had told him that he would be out of a job for six months and survive without emotional damage he would have thought they were crazy. During this time, he had consistently practiced training his mind and body with my Beta Relaxation CD. It had helped him to relax and enjoy his environment, relationships, and everything he held dear in his life. He said that being out of work had not been an intense anxiety experience; rather, he felt enriched by the time off. He said the feelings that arose while learning how to relax changed his whole perception of himself and the world. He experienced a true sense of joy and of being blessed, and knew he was lucky for all that he had in life. This joyful sense of being continued in his new job as a senior executive in a Fortune 50 company, and he didn't want it to wear off. I told him if he kept practicing and developing his brain-mind connection, it would only get better.

When we are in balance, beta's electrical activity is the intense energy that sparks clear thinking so that we can analyze problems and conceptualize new possible outcomes. It also allows us to make plans or set goals for the future, as well as figure out the impact of past actions. Beta is essential in making "executive decisions" in the prefrontal lobe of the brain to give basic direction and guidance in our daily lives. These decisions come from the conscious level of awareness rather than the unconscious.

Our ability to make discriminating judgments that can initiate positive growth in our lives and even save us from harm is housed in the prefrontal lobe and is indicated by beta-wave activity. Beta can also reflect the negative judgment maker in the prefrontal lobe that criticizes others as well as ourselves. These positive and negative judging qualities are developed by age twelve, and by the time we are in our twenties, our judgment and discretion are fully mature. Until this point of full brain development, our parents theoretically act as models for the best way to be in the world. Making a judgment cannot be executed without the ability to focus, concentrate, or hold our attention on a particular issue. This judging quality is what distinguishes us from our lower level ancestors. Our ability to focus our attention and to make changes and judgments is how we adapt to stay alive. The power of the prefrontal lobe mind tools—intention, attention, receptivity, and awareness—connect the neocortex, the limbic center, and the reptilian brain.

On my first three-month meditation retreat, I began to dislike the woman who sat next to me in the auditorium as we meditated hour after hour in silence for ten hours a day. My dislike stemmed from her being so pretty and wearing the best and most stylish clothes of anyone at the retreat. Every day she wore a new coordinated outfit. I could not compete. I was actually relieved when she left after six weeks. But I soon realized that I had been projecting my own mind stuff on her. From that point on, I watched my reactions of competition, judgment, and of feeling sorry for myself. I began to see how much stress and suffering it brought me. I paid closer attention to these negative qualities in myself as they arose in my mind. As I kept watching and observing them, they began to have less impact on my mind. I was receptive to the new insight and feeling of change in me. As a result, a new awareness began to form in my mind: Exploring the inner self with strong commitment and self-observation has the power to produce significant change in one's life. From the work I've done over the years with EEG monitoring, I am sure my beta waves were reduced. I gained insights about being reprimanded as a child if I was not dressed "appropriately." During those long days of mind training in the meditation hall, I worked to release the old programming that influenced my judgments.

Enneagram Defense Patterns

How you defend yourself or resist an attack by others or by your own mind can be seen in your Enneagram pattern. What the pattern of your type shows is your orientation to judging or being judged and how you defend yourself. Note your type's pattern in the following and explore how your defense orientation operates in you.

- **One** is the reformer; defends by projecting judgment onto something or someone.
- **Two** is the caregiver; defends by repressing his/her own needs with self-sacrifice.
- **Three** is the achiever; defends as a workaholic identifying with his/her role.

- **Four** is the individualist; defends by taking on others' feelings as his/her own.

- **Five** is the investigator; defends by withdrawing into isolation to recharge.

- **Six** is the loyalist; defends by feeling betrayed and abandoned.

- **Seven** is the adventurer; defends by rationalization, strategizing, and planning.

- **Eight** is the challenger; defends by denial, guilt-tripping, and projecting blame onto others.

- **Nine** is the peacemaker; defends by going numb and unconscious to suppress the rage.

Defense patterns show up strongly in personal and professional relationships, and most obviously in the spousal/partner relationship. Mike and Sandra, an executive couple, spent two days with me to unravel the stress and dysfunction in their relationship. It was clear to me from the phone conversation we had prior to their coming that their marriage was at a critical juncture. I used assessments to identify their Enneagram personality types; Mike is a five and Sandra an eight. I had them take the Braverman neurotransmitter assessment test to determine the levels of neurotransmitters in their brains and profiled their brain-wave patterns on the Brain Mirror. I then created individual relaxation meditation practices for each of them. As a VP of marketing, Mike is a frequent business traveler, leaving Sandra, who is an executive in a local company, to contend with their three young boys. In a private session, she acknowledged her angry reaction at being "deserted" and was concerned that she was projecting it onto her boys. This had intensified since they had begun remodeling their home. And the more Mike traveled, the more Sandra felt like she was raising her boys alone. For an Enneagram 8, anger is one of the key emotions to resolve.

As Sandra began to use my Beta Relaxation CD every morning and before she went to bed, her comments were insightful: "I could see the effects of the practice. As it reduced my angry reactions together with the intention to be more loving, I began to feel a bond with my boys and with Mike." We worked on this issue as we brought her beta waves back into balance and repatterned the hardwired reaction. There were many other issues we dealt with in those two days, but this private session was a turning point for her in acknowledging and dealing with her anger and being able to talk calmly about her reactions with her husband. Being an Enneagram 5, Mike was able to listen to Sandra's concerns without withdrawing and disconnecting from her. They were able to resolve issues in such a way that was satisfying to both of them and to their family.

Beta brain waves carry the automatic thoughts that are our beliefs and attitudes about ourselves. These continually run through our minds and make up our day-to-day personality and identity. When negative, these preprogrammed automatic thoughts block our Flow and can control our reactions, responses, and behaviors. Beta also generates the pleasures and addictions in our reward center, which rewards us with pleasure, particularly from what we eat and through sexual activity. The reward center monitors feelings of pleasure and non-pleasure. There are also many external chemicals we ingest that influence and produce the beta-wave state. Stimulants such as sugar, alcohol, nicotine, caffeine (in coffee, tea, and soft drinks), diet pills, and amphetamines can overamplify that feeling of pleasure, but chronic use depletes beta waves. When they are depleted, we dip down into low beta states. Attention deficit is a behavior pattern associated with the low state, which is why we will take these stimulants to get us back to what feels normal for us.

Terry is an Enneagram 5 and had a stressful job situation. At work, he felt as if he was being attacked. He would withdraw in response and was therefore not present to the situation. As manager of strategy development, he worked twelve hours a day, but said his supervisor and coworkers did not appreciate his contributions. He felt he was not good enough, a failure, which worried him continually. His position necessitated a strong, clear, alertly thinking mind. I found his beta brain-wave activity low, even with his anxious thoughts and history as a strategic thinker. I asked him if he was low on energy, and he said he was, to the point of zoning out in front of the TV at night.

To get started in the morning, he drank four cups of coffee, and to keep himself going during the day, he took cigarette breaks and drank energy drinks in the afternoon when he got sleepy. He further revealed a family history of alcoholism, and though he did not drink alcohol, he smoked, drank coffee, and ate sweets to get energy. The Braverman neurotransmitter assessment test revealed that his dopamine was very deficient, which accounted for the low beta-wave pattern and the attempt to boost himself with stimulants. Terry began to change his stimulant input and to focus on a walking meditation practice to increase beta waves and bring up his dopamine levels. The result was he found he was spending much less time watching TV and more time with enthusiasm working on a home building project. His situation at work also improved.

About Dopamine

Dopamine, the chemical energy of beta waves, has a huge influence on shaping your personality. It charges your energy voltage through your metabolism. The by-product of dopamine is adrenaline, the hormone involved in the fight-or-flight response, which can also be called the fear-flight response. In this chronic stress situation, you may be overly anxious due to the accumulation of adrenaline or cortisol in your system. You may also procrastinate, be careless in relationships or not engage in close ones, and have a decreased libido and poor self-image. You will also tend to seek pleasure by absorption in hobbies, food, TV, and so forth. The tendency of this self-absorption is to become isolated and separated from others.

When you are chemically charged with a healthy level of dopamine, you are on top of everything. You relish your sexual relations, your food tastes fantastic, and everything is a source of pleasure for you. The foods that are energy boosting for dopamine are broccoli, carrots, egg whites, salmon, pomegranate juice, spinach, and unsalted almonds. Some teas that boost dopamine are green tea, oolong tea, white tea, and rooibos tea. Spices, herbs, and flavorful foods that will boost your metabolism, which dopamine monitors, are flaxseed, garlic, green tea, mustard seed, onion, stevia, and yarrow. Some supplements that boost beta brain energies are Ginkgo biloba, B complex, tyrosine, and phenylalanine.

Beta Ranges

Understanding the ranges of beta-wave energy can help you determine if there is too much or too little of it occurring in your brain. In the high beta frequency range (18–38 Hz), if you have too much, your mind is a constant flutter of chatter. This is what is called the "monkey mind." In this frequency range, you will find it difficult to shut off your mental chatter. You are generally filled with intense worry and high anxiety, as well as depression. The characteristics of a person in this state include intense drive, competitiveness, impulsivity, anxiety, and even terror. This person has high-frequency and high-volume brain waves. As I described earlier, the fight-or-flight syndrome is connected to the neurotransmitter dopamine with its by-product of adrenaline. This combination increases blood flow and pulse rate. So high-frequency, high-volume beta brain waves are an indicator that you need to relax the body, call it to rest, and allow it to reset.

When you have such a high level of anxiety, you need something to calm you down. So at the end of the day, you might take an alcoholic drink or a prescription drug to calm your frenzied mind. With both dopamine and adrenaline already coursing through your system, adding another drug can generate addiction upon addiction—that is, an increasing dependence on both internal and external stimulants to maintain your life.

In midrange beta (15–18 Hz), there is a slowing down of intensity. This midrange permits a clearer awareness of yourself and your surroundings through self-observation. In this range, you still have a strong mental focus and are alert and active but not agitated.

Beta brain wave frequency and volume in the low range (12–15 Hz) is called sensory motor rhythm (SMR), and it is associated with relaxed, yet focused behavior and attention skills. SMR frequencies make people feel more present and in the immediate moment. In this range, the busy mind has slowed down considerably and these frequencies have the capacity to focus, process information, and perform tasks.

SMR aids us in better utilizing the mental abilities we already have and to increase the quality of one's intelligence. In this state, you are alert, able to focus, and concentrate. This part of the brain is responsible for communicating to the muscular and skeletal systems. When the SMR frequencies of brain waves are not optimally proportional to the other brain waves in the beta area, the communication between the brain and the motor systems of the body becomes skewed. As a result, a person's mind wanders and becomes scattered, making it difficult to hold a concentrated edge in conversations, reading, or problem solving. These conditions may indicate that a person has attention deficit disorder (ADD) or simply a general lack of focused attention. The skewed mental-motor communication can also exacerbate chronic dysfunction of any muscle groups that are in pain, as in fibromyalgia. People who have attention-deficit/hyperactivity disorder (ADHD) and others who are generally hyperactive have low SMR beta-wave activity and are therefore not getting enough stimulation. They tend to be very physically active and seek external stimulation as a means of increasing SMR beta waves.

A lack of body movement or some form of restraint on body movement can lower the SMR frequency. People who suffer from low-frequency beta activity often grab a quick cup of coffee or a cigarette but more likely a sugar treat to activate a higher beta frequency state. Beta brain waves can also increase if your body is tense with chronic stress. As a result, blood pressure rises, muscular pain or tension increases, and chronic fatigue and digestive problems can occur, along with sugar craving.

It is a tradition to sit still in meditation so that the effect of relaxation is not interrupted and the mind remains alert. The low-frequency range of beta brings difficulty with self-discipline, particularly if you want to meditate. Mind training is one antidote to lower beta states. It can increase sensory motor rhythm, produce a relaxed focus, and improve attentive abilities that can move you out of the low beta frequency. Neurofeedback practitioners have found that when there is low SMR activity in people with learning disabilities, epilepsy, depression, bipolar, Asperger's, and autism, these individuals can increase the frequency of beta brain waves using neurofeedback or biofeedback technology.

There is a wave frequency between alpha and beta (12–23 Hz) that monitors the body. This range regulates the circadian rhythms of the body such as sleep cycles, as well as breathing, voluntary muscles, blood pressure, and sugar levels. We know that when the beta activity is too much or too little we are either too excitable or too dull. In both the high and low beta ranges, our bodily functions suffer.

Balancing Beta

I noted earlier the foods that balance beta, but exercise is also critical. Beta brain waves are supported by both aerobic and anaerobic exercise. Balance your exercise program with aerobic activities such as daily walks, swimming, bike riding, dancing, and running. If you are a professional that travels a lot, learn some basic yoga postures that you can do in a hotel room. Everyone needs to take a walk at least once a day, not only to exercise the body, but also simply to connect our minds with nature. Anti-aerobic activity includes weight training for muscle and bone, particularly as we grow older. Creative and relaxation exercises are a huge balance function for beta. Do things regularly that are fun for you. Hobbies like gardening, painting, writing, photography, woodworking, sewing, and knitting bring beta into natural balance.

There is an anomaly about very high beta waves. Another wave frequency has been identified within that range. Gamma waves are not a distinct brain-wave class, but are generally placed into the higher beta-wave category. They have been a focus of the Tibetan monks' meditation research project conducted by Richard Davidson at the University of Wisconsin. These long-term Buddhist meditators displayed high amounts of gamma waves in the left frontal cortex during meditation. The distinguishing characteristic of gamma waves is that they are continuously present during fast, low-voltage to high-voltage neocortical activity, which can occur during sleep in the rapid eye movement (REM) stage, as well as in altered states of consciousness.

Gamma waves are produced when neurons emit electrical signals in the frequency range of 5–70 Hz. This finding suggests that gamma rhythms may be organized in such a way as to sweep across the whole brain. They seem to synthesize bits of individual information and fuse them together. There is the possibility that they are temporarily holding together a single cognitive experience. For example, if you are looking at an automobile, you might notice its color, design, shape, and interior textures. These characteristics are all perceived and processed by different parts of the brain, and could be expressed in the activation of gamma rhythms. It is also held that gamma and theta brain waves work together to package brain information into consistent images, thoughts, and memories. The meditation research found gamma waves unify information associated with being self-aware, highly conceptual, and acutely perceptive. The gamma waves are stimulated through repetitive meditation practice. They also appear in 40 Hz sensory responses and increase when we pay attention but disappear with loss of consciousness during anesthesia. A repetitive auditory and visual stimulation (for example, meditation that combines both chanting and visualization) at 40 Hz can generate a large steady 40 Hz gamma response. When this occurs, the mind is vibrant, insightful, highly intuitive, and blissful; some people even have out-of-body experiences.

The signs of an untrained mind described by Buddha actually reflect extreme high and low beta energies. The first step to working consciously with beta brain-wave balance is to train the mind. Here, we will apply the functions of breath and muscle relaxation to train the beta brain-mind pattern to serve us.

The nervous system regards relaxation of the voluntary muscles as the way to reduce tension, and beta is involved in maintaining the voluntary muscles. When beta is in balance, the muscles are healthy and respond when we need them. If they are unhealthy, they can become dysfunctional, which can even result in Parkinson's disease. Breath and relaxation bring balance by allowing the stress hormones to be eliminated from the body and returning the system to stability and integration.

Here are key things to remember and repeat to yourself when your mind races out of control or gets attached or obsessed, when it seems impossible to stop the chatter, or when it simply becomes impossible to focus. I've put them in the form of self-statements to use when your mind won't stop.

Here is a set of self-affirming statements for use with the beta-state exercises. You can use any of the statements as you need them, but there is one statement that applies to your Enneagram type. It is helpful if you say the statement a few times before and after you meditate.

- I am free of stress to focus my attention and change my consciousness.

- I have self-control and self-discipline to direct my intention and focus my attention.

- I release anxiety and worry, and my heart rate and blood pressure go down.

- I breathe slowly and connect with my vagus nerve to relax and reset my body. (Note: The vagus nerve starts in the brain stem and sends information to the lungs, heart, and digestive system, among others.)

- I breathe in a short breath and exhale a long breath to stimulate the autonomic nervous system (ANS).

- I know that stress hormones are accumulating around the nerve synapses, and as I relax they are released to give me a healthy body and stable mind.

- As I reduce my stress, my brain hemispheres are in balance.

- Lowering beta waves, I reduce anxiety and increase muscular activity.

Beta Exercises

Thought Environment

The intention of this exercise is to become aware of the thought environment in which you live and to detach from it. Set a timer for five minutes.

1. Find a comfortable place to sit in a quiet undisturbed environment.

2. With your eyes closed, bring your attention to your breath.

3. Let your breath be relaxed and natural.

4. Notice the sequence of thoughts in your mind. Simply observe them.

5. Notice which thoughts you tend to hold on to, think about, fantasize, etc.

6. Imagine a windy day and your thoughts are like leaves being blown and disappearing into the atmosphere above you. As thoughts come and go, keep having the wind blow them away.

7. When the timer goes off, sit and contemplate the kinds of thought you had that kept coming and going.

8. Journaling:

Describe the kinds of thoughts you had:

Planning_____

Blaming_____

Judging_____

Memories _____

Emotional_____

Care of Others _____

Analyzing_____

Doubting_____

Do your thoughts match your Enneagram personality type?

What happened to your thoughts when the wind blew into the sky?

Concentration

The intention of this exercise is to focus your mind. You do this by placing your attention on your breath. It is a good exercise to return to when you are sleepy, particularly in meditation. It can quickly bring you to an aware, focused state—a lifesaver when you are in a lethargic slump.

1. Find a comfortable place to sit in a quiet undisturbed environment.

2. Close your eyes and bring your attention to your breath.

3. On your first inhalation, say 1 to yourself. On your next inhalation, say 2 to yourself. Continue the count until you have reached ten inhalations, and then repeat five times for a total of fifty inhalations. Bringing more oxygen into your system consciously will pep you up.

Breath Observation

The intention of this exercise is to become aware of the subtleness of your breath, which will naturally begin to relax your body. Set a timer for seven minutes.

1. Find a comfortable place to sit in a quiet undisturbed environment.

2. With your eyes closed, bring your attention to your breath.

3. Let your breath be relaxed and natural.

4. Do not attempt to control your breath—follow it, do not force it.

5. Be aware of the sensations and rhythms of your breath. Observe.

6. Notice when your breath is either long or short on the inhalation or exhalation.

7. Become aware of the resting spots of your mind when observing your breath. Does your mind go to the tip of your nose, middle of your head, palate, base of your throat, breastbone (sternum), belly, or where?

Beta Relaxation Meditation

For the Beta Relaxation Meditation, you will combine the way the brain works with the four prefrontal cortex mind faculties as your tools. The key questions of the faculties are: *What is my intention? Where do I put my attention? When am I receptive? How am I aware?* The Beta Relaxation Meditation table gives examples of answers to these questions that you might encounter as you begin the beta meditation practice. You can use the table as a guideline for setting your intention for the practice and for where you will focus your attention.

Beta Relaxation Meditation: Mind Tools & Guidelines

Intention	Attention	Receptivity/ Awareness
To slow my thoughts and relax my body.	The narrow objective focus is on the breath and body muscles. No need to control, force, or evaluate. As you inhale, your attention is on the muscle region; as you exhale, your attention is on relaxing the muscles. Aim and sustain if thoughts arise, and go back to the breath and the relaxation.	Difficulty of stilling the mind. Difficulty in relaxing the muscles. Mind filled with everyday affairs. Attention not sustained. Occasional nausea. Beginning to feel calmed down and relaxed. Drifting off to sleep. Mind increasingly quiet, centered, and concentrated.

Preparation

The most important meditation preparation is to be in a place where it is quiet and where you will not be disturbed by the phone, animals, or another person. Find a comfortable chair or meditation pillow to sit on. If seated in a chair, have your feet on the floor. If on a pillow, sit in a cross-legged meditation style on the floor. It is best not to lie down to meditate, as the mind will tend to relax too much, and you will have the tendency to fall asleep.

As you sit, your back and spine need to be straight and your arms loose at your sides. Rest your hands, palms down, on your thighs. As you settle into your sitting position, focus your gaze directly in front of you so that when you close your eyes (or drop your gaze), your head and shoulders will be relaxed. If possible, sit in the same location each time you meditate.

Meditation

As you practice the Beta Relaxation Meditation, give yourself enough time to breathe, relax, and let go. If you find you need further direction to relax or want to be guided in this meditation, you can download the CD for it (see appendix). Let us begin.

1. Close your eyes...Begin by listening to the sounds in your environment...notice what they are...and where they are coming from...Permit yourself to feel comfortable and content in your surroundings.

2. Bring your attention to your eyes...see or feel the tiny muscles around your eyes and allow them to relax and soften. Your eyes bring information to you, but now shift their attention from the outside to turning their attention inward...

3. Let the relaxing, softening quality filter from behind your eyes and flow into the brain cavity and into your scalp...

4. From your scalp, move the softening quality to your face and experience your forehead becoming spacious, open, and relaxed...

5. Relax the rest of your face, including your nose and cheeks. Feel them become smooth and relaxed...

6. Notice your lips...Open your lips slightly, dropping any tension.

7. Notice both the top and bottom of your tongue and let it soften so that it floats in your mouth cavity. This reduces the amount of self-talk.

8. Allow your jaws where they connect to the mouth cavity to gently drop, reducing any tightness.

9. As the jaws soften, the neck and shoulders begin to drop and relax as well.

10. Let the flow of softness float down your right arm and into your hand and fingers...

11. Notice the difference between your arms...Now relax your left arm, then your hand and fingers...Notice how both arms become heavy...with this relaxation there is no need to hold on.

12. When you are ready, move to your upper torso and your chest and soften and relax your diaphragm...

13. Move to your back and to the top of your spine at the base of your neck...gradually move down your spine, softening and relaxing the muscles in your back...

14. Include the buttocks and the pelvic floor in the relaxing and softening until your entire spine feels connected...and relaxed...

15. Let go of any tension and relax the belly...pelvis...hips...the center of your body...

16. Let the flow of gentle relaxation move into your right thigh down into your calf...feet...toes...

17. Notice the difference between your legs. Now, begin to soften your left thigh and then your calf...feet...toes...

18. Hold your next inhalation and scan your body from the bottom of your feet up your legs, abdomen, upper torso, shoulders, arms

neck, face, and head. As you exhale, let go of any remaining tension in your body...

19. Take two more breaths as you scan and relax...

20. Be fully aware of this deep relaxation...notice your breath gently moving in and out of your nose...

21. If you choose, allow a feeling, symbol, or image to arise to act as a marker of this deep state of relaxation...This marker can remind you of this state at any time.

22. Now gently bring yourself back to feel where you are sitting or lying. Take several deep breaths. Open your eyes and stretch your body. Before you get up, notice how you feel refreshed and alert. Continue to feel this state of relaxation moment-to-moment in your daily activities.

23. Journal your experience so that you can observe your development as you go deeper each time you repeat this meditation.

Journaling Your Progress

Practice Beta Relaxation Meditation daily for a week. After each practice session, answer questions on your progress in quieting the mind and relaxing your body. You can copy the Beta Journal on the next page to use in recording your answers. Only answer the questions that are applicable to your experience in each session.

Beta Relaxation Meditation Journal

Date:

Mental Tools: Intention, Attention, Receptivity, Awareness

Were you aware of the feeling sounds in the room as well as outside? Describe.

What kinds of thoughts were moving through your mind? List. How many thoughts? When did they start to decrease or did they?

Describe how you followed your breath. Were you following its rhythm at the belly or in the chest area, or at the entrance to the nose?

What did it feel like to relax your jaw and tongue? What difference did it make in relation to your body and mind?

What was it like to sustain your attention on your inhale and exhale as you relaxed each muscle region?

What did the relaxation feel like in each muscle region?

Which muscle region area was the easiest and which area was the most difficult to relax?

Describe what your mind and muscles were like at the end of the relaxation?

What was the felt sense, word, or image that reflects the body and mind being completely relaxed?

In the Thought Environment exercise, you noticed that when you closed your eyes and became aware of your "monkey mind," your thoughts were jumping from one thought to another and from one subject to another. It has been reported that we have approximately sixty thousand thoughts a day. Something new can only come as we focus our intention on what we really want to experience. Comedian Eddie Cantor once said, "It's not only the scenery you miss by going too fast—you also miss the sense of where you are going and why."

People with high-amplitude beta brain waves tend to become narrowly focused, which results in being self-centered about themselves and the people and situations around them. As dopamine becomes depleted, their life's focus gets constricted and they become so emotionally intense that they seem to be "strangling" themselves. In this high beta state, their minds are out of balance and they are not in harmony with themselves or in relationships, nor moving in rhythm with their lives. They are caught in a prison, and the only way out for the conscious mind and brain is through the body.

Through consciously relaxing tense muscles and observing your breath moving in and out, these incessant thoughts can be quickly reduced. You can do this when you are driving, standing in line at the grocery store, or sitting in a doctor's reception room. The practice is very simple. As you move your attention to your breath, begin to notice the strongest body tension. As you inhale, focus on the tense area. As you exhale, release the tension. Next scan your body and let each inhalation and exhalation relax any tightness in the shoulders, eyes, jaw, and so on. Take a moment and do this exercise as you read this book. This breathing slows down the beta waves and lets you focus more easily even as you continue to read.

No matter what your personal challenges, you don't have to let the beta brain pattern constantly speed up your life. You can begin to change that right now as you keep up this practice through the whole day. There is much more to life than a stream of rationalizations and justifications. Learning to make friends with beta and having it serve you is the doorway to your liberation.

As you've seen, the beta brain waves in the prefrontal lobe of the neocortex function to focus your mind; it is your means of self-reflection and the source of self-awareness. This ability to concentrate the mind can become the most powerful force we know, if we learn to use it. Developing concentration in beta brain waves is similar to the challenge of learning a new subject. To master the subject, you must put your full attention to work. And to excel, you must hone that concentration to a fine point. If you observe Tiger Woods as he walks from one shot to the next, he doesn't look at or talk to other players. Rather he is inwardly focused, eyes down, concentrating on his next shot.

If you train your mind to be focused, rather than leaving it to random, strangling thoughts, your conscious awareness can join together the neocortex, the limbic brain, and the reptilian brain into an integrated consciousness. As an analogy, steam, water, and ice are the same substance, only in different states. As the outer temperature rises or drops, these different states are derived one from the other. But it all starts with the same liquid, H2O. Brain waves are also affected by inner and outer circumstances. In this analogy, the beta brain wave is steam, its molecules in the most active or excitable state. You must first work with the beta brain waves to slow the molecules, that is, focus and relax the muscles. This allows your mind to slow down and prepare you for the next leg of your journey of consciousness: alpha brain waves.

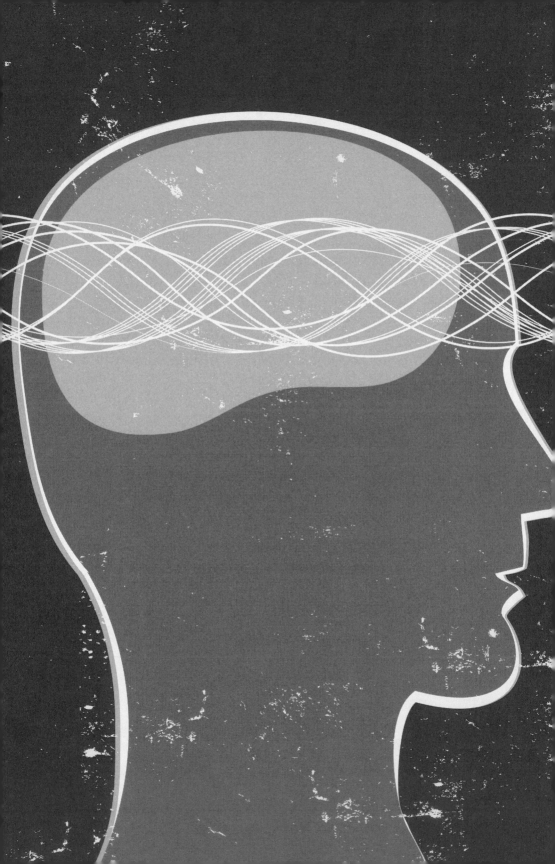

6

Alpha Brain Waves
and Acetylcholine

*One may be surrounded by great beauty, by mountains and fields
and rivers. But unless one is alive to it all, one might just as well be
dead.*

—Jiddu Krishnamurti

As the meditation class arrives at the door of my meditation cottage to experience and learn the function of their alpha brain waves, I immediately redirect them to follow my drumbeat into the garden. Step-by-step we go as I instruct them to use as many of their five senses as possible. I encourage them to see the colors of the flowers, smell the plants and earth, feel the breeze, hear the birds, note the rustling of the leaves, and taste an herb. I want them to just let their senses explore their environment and totally immerse themselves into the richness of the world around them. People move slowly in different directions throughout the garden. Some stop and stand with heads tilted, listen with eyes closed to the sounds of bees and the breeze moving through the trees. Others bend down to look into the center of flowers. Still others sit on the ground, holding stones in their hands and stroking the plants near them. My hope is that every person will feel their inner silence as they let the worries, struggles, and fears of their lives dissolve into nature.

Later, as we silently gather in the cottage, I let them settle in before I ask, "What happened to you as you let yourself surrender to the outer world of sensations?" The responses are astounding and yet are met with nods of agreement. Various ones answer that they feel relaxed, at peace, and revitalized. They go on to say that a load has been lifted from their shoulders and they feel lighter, and at the same time they feel grounded and centered. This shift of feeling happened in a short ten minutes of consciously exploring with the sensations of the body the world around them.

What is it that in just a few minutes can change a whole mindset? We live in a world that compounds our stress, fear, and uncertainty. What we call our normal mind is our crazy mind. It is a mind super-charged by our own mental and emotional intensity. Turning inward, each of us finds our own way to the place of relaxation, calm, peace, and inner freedom—the home base on which we can absolutely rely. Finding our home base shows us that we have a choice about the load of stress and suffering we carry, that we can, in fact, reduce it in less than ten minutes if we know the tools to use.

The beta brain-wave state is like a busy city with its excitement and vitality, but the alpha brain-wave state is like being in a beautiful countryside with the constant physical sensations of the sound of birds singing and water bubbling in a stream, the sight of every shade of green imaginable, the warmth of sun on your skin, and just the right amount of breeze gently brushing your face. In an alpha state, you feel the stability of solid earth and feel present with yourself as your thoughts settle into the calm, alive physicality of a countryside's sensual nature.

Alpha electrical pulses carry a continuous uninterrupted momentum of thoughts like the complex continuity of nature's qualities. One of my clients, James, an Enneagram 8, made the remark when he started out with my mind-training program that "my mind is like a wild horse with thoughts racing too fast." He admitted he was not disciplined, often controlled by his anger, and was easily distracted from real-time commitments for months at a time. Now, after three years of meditating and working with other mind tools, and not judging himself for being inconsistent, he can quiet his mind by just closing his eyes. He says after three years of practice, "Knowing how to bring my mind into focus is a gift when I choose to use it. Whenever I do focus my mind, it changes my life in some tangible way." With this persistence of practice, his mind became a gentle well-mannered thoroughbred.

In our hand model of the brain, alpha brain waves occur at the knuckles on top of your closed hand. They extend from the thalamus at the top of the brain stem into the neocortex. They provide the connection between external bodily sensations and their interpretation by the brain. Thus alpha mediates conscious sensual experience. Alpha waves move physical sensation information throughout the brain and give you the kinesthetic experience of the smooth texture of silk and the heat from the sun on your skin, the auditory experience of the sound of waterfalls or the honking of a car horn, and so on through the five senses. All of these sensations filter through the relay station in the parietal lobe of the cortex and are dispersed to the rest of the brain and body. We can only know physical reality through our sensations. Alpha enables us to feel grounded in our bodies and solidly affixed to the earth. Alpha brain waves are the core to knowing we are alive and to being fully in the present moment, or as Eckhart Tolle calls it, "the Power of Now."

One of the main roles of alpha waves is to process and regulate the rate of sensory information coming at us. We would go crazy with all this stimuli if it weren't regulated. Alpha brain function enables us to pay attention to certain sensations and not to others. Physics demonstrates that a range of vital electric and magnetic fields across the electromagnetic spectrum surround and interpenetrate the human body. This spectrum is filled with vibrations that affect our body and brain from the high frequencies of gamma rays, X rays, and ultraviolet light to the low frequencies of infrared radiation, microwaves, and radio waves. This is a vast range with the visible light and the sound spectrum in the middle. By comparison to the overall electromagnetic spectrum, the physical reality we experience occurs within a very narrow range of frequencies, and we are only conscious of a very small amount of it.

The various types of meditation practices that have been methodically passed down to us through the ages demonstrate that we can develop a greater sensitivity to the broader electromagnetic spectrum. It is in an alpha state that we begin to observe our actual experience of physical sensations moment to moment. In this monitoring, we experience the space from which these sensations arise in our conscious awareness. Alpha is the doorway to this experience.

In mind training, we use physical sensations as an object of attention to slow our thoughts but stay in touch with the physicality of our aliveness. The Buddhists call this practice "mindfulness," which is the conscious attention to everything that is occurring in our awareness moment to moment. Mindfulness is noting the sensations of our hand turning a door handle, lifting our feet and returning them to earth as we walk, picking up a fork and slowly placing a bite of food in our mouth. It is also noticing the heat of the sun on one side of our face and the slight coolness on the other side in the sun's shadow. Learning to use alpha to focus your attention is key to mindfulness practice.

Enneagram Attention Patterns

The Enneagram shows you where the propensity of your personality type automatically places your attention. Knowing this automatic tendency gives you insight in how to develop your attention more effectively, and shows both your strength and your weakness. Remember, "Where you put your attention is who you are." Your attention to both internal and external stimuli may become so attached that it blocks deepening the meditative state or mind training. The following list indicates where the nine Enneagram types tend to become preoccupied and attached and place their attention.

1. **One** is the reformer; attention to the logic of right and wrong.

2. **Two** is the caregiver; attention to helping others and relationships.

3. **Three** is an achiever; attention to using deceit to reach his/her goals.

4. **Four** is an individualist; attention to his/her feelings by fantasizing.

5. **Five** is an investigator; attention to mastering ideas by knowing how things work.

6. **Six** is the loyalist; attention to worry about being safe and secure.

7. **Seven** is the adventurer; attention to what next to do by planning.

8. **Eight** is the challenger; attention to control by being objective.

9. **Nine** is the peacemaker; attention to harmony by being comfortable.

Contemplate from your Enneagram type where you tend to focus attention. This is generally unconscious, but the list is to help you become more observant of the focus of your attention. For example, the tendency of an Enneagram 1 in conversation and in confronting problems and issues is to focus his attention on what's right or wrong in the situation, with other people or with himself. As an Enneagram 6, I have the tendency to scan my environment constantly to determine whether it is safe for me physically, emotionally, professionally, and so on. After years of practice, when I notice this happening, my self-observation allows me to shift my attention and focus to other things in my environment that expand with my conscious awareness. As noted previously, your Enneagram type only reflects your fundamental patterns, and you can train yourself through self-observation and mind practice not to be unconsciously controlled by them.

Being attentive to the physical experience of hearing, seeing, feeling, touching, and tasting allows you to tune into the space that surrounds each sensation. Let me explain. Your body occupies space, or has volume that takes up space, as you sit reading this book. If you focus your attention, you can distinguish between the space your body occupies and the space of the room in which you are sitting. The attention placed on your bodily sensations received from the space your body occupies begins to alter your perception of yourself, and it is one of the fastest ways to move into the experience of the present moment. When you are able to experience the outer sensations of sound, light, touch, and so forth as connected inside your body, there is an experience of being in space.

Let me give you an example. A man named Scott, an Enneagram 1, is in one of my meditation circles. For several weeks in his practice, he had been working on shifting his attention from thinking about the busy external world to the inner world of sensations. As I guided the group into relaxation, he later reported that his body became extremely relaxed and his mind was able to release the mental chatter. At first he was amazed at how clear and peaceful he felt. I next guided the group to scan their bodies. His attention went to his shoulders, and he immediately experienced a gentle buzzing sensation there. This is where he holds tension. As he kept his attention focused on the buzzing sound of the tension, he noticed his shoulders relaxing. As he focused more deeply on the relaxation, the buzzing began to subside. What happened next startled him. As the sound began to fade, he discovered that not only was the tension dissolving in his body, but the tension seemed to dissolve into pure space as well. He appeared to be floating in what he could only describe as a sea of incredible peace. He then understood that every sensation is surrounded by and rests in space. As he paid attention to the sensations of touch and sound, they returned to the space from which they arose. He said, "I understood I was in a place of healing."

This meditation was a powerful shift for an Enneagram 1. Letting go of the judging mind's attention on whether he was in the right sitting position, or if he should move his shoulder to change the position, he simply put his full attention on the sound sensation of his shoulder and experienced a new way to heal himself.

Speed of thought functions through alpha brain waves. We have all met the fast talker who jumps from subject to subject. I call this type the "quick thinker." By knowing how to focus this speed of alpha, anyone can become a "quick thinker" naturally. Developing your alpha frequency allows this quickness of mind to connect pieces instantly to make a comprehensive whole. The quick thinker sees fantastic imagery, creates a piece of music or poetry, generates innovative ideas, uses creative language, and loves communication interaction. Learning to slow your alpha waves also provides a different way to access information and gain insight.

Dave, another Enneagram 1, has been vigilant in training his mind to slow his thoughts so he can be more aware of the nonrational insights and intuitive connections on which he acts. In one session, he told me about his experience driving to the post office. On the way he kept getting the "message" to go to a certain café in town that arose as a picture in his mind of the café. He had other plans after he went to the post office but said to himself "Why not?" and drove a few blocks to the café. As Dave walked in, a friend rushed up to greet him and said that she and another friend had just been talking about him. They wanted him to answer a question that only he could answer. They were going to call him on their cell phone but he showed up at exactly the right moment. Was this a mere coincidence? Perhaps it was, but alpha waves with their intuitive connection can be a source of intuitive knowing. Many people who learn to focus attention and develop their alpha state find this a common experience.

As we grow older, we become habituated to our sensations and lose touch with this living reality of our being. We recognize a tree, but on some level we don't really see it anymore. We feel we waste time stopping and listening to the song of a bird or observing the quivering leaves in a tree. We rarely pause to see the changing colors of nature and the movement of the clouds in the sky. Nor do we notice the chant of the crickets. We have more important things to do. With that attitude, we lose touch with the wondrous life around us. Our thoughts are the chants of a never-ending stream that absorbs us and distances us from our physical surroundings. We fail to see its beauty and miss the essence of this life.

Given the ever-demanding cultural environment around us, it is important to develop and become attentive to nature, which is our source and what brings aliveness to us. It is the gateway to a deeper form of meditation, and without the awareness of our sensations, meditation stays at a superficial level. Alpha mental patterns use sensations to envision, imagine, and create something new. For example, alpha enables you to visualize a new house and have all the sensations of color, form, and feelings of what it would feel like to be in that house. Alpha is what gives power to your intention to create a positive future and to actually manifest it.

Acetylcholine

The neurotransmitter acetylcholine is the alpha brain-wave partner to keep brain information moving throughout the body-brain. It is a lubricant of the myelin sheath around the nerves so that the information that travels across the nerve gap doesn't get lost upon arrival at its destination. It helps keep the speed of your thoughts in motion as information is sent across the neurons. People who think and talk fast are demonstrating how acetylcholine works. Acetylcholine helps us remember what we are saying and doing. Thus, it juices the mind to be flexible, quick in movement, creative, and innovative. It also serves to increase our intuition, language skills, and memory retention.

The foods that replenish acetylcholine and help alpha brain waves stay in balance are: avocado, cucumber, zucchini, lettuce, nuts, milk products (whole and skim milk, cream, ice cream, sour cream), eggs (fried, poached, or baked), luncheon meats and sausages, liver, beef, and olive oil salad dressings. Note that many of these foods are fat-based. Alpha needs natural fats for balanced activity. We crave foods with fat because they deliver a choline boost to our brains.

Too Much or Too Little

The right brain is most active when alpha brain waves are activated, and the left brain is most active when beta brain waves are activated. The hemispheres, with their respective brain waves, must work together to form a harmonious balance in order for us to experience calm awareness. Alpha brain-wave patterns involve a functional shift away from a linguistic conceptual facility toward the nonverbal imagery and somatic sensation of the right hemisphere. The 1960s made this state of mind notorious when it was found that smoking marijuana induced it, but marijuana is only a substitute for the alpha-wave state. Research demonstrates that smoking marijuana puts the mind in the present moment, aware and calm. When we are in healthy alpha rhythm, this addictive need disappears because we naturally have a sense of calmness. In alpha, it is easy to learn and see the world as it exists.

Alpha brain patterns are generally increased when your eyes are closed. If too much alpha is produced, some people find it hard to focus and concentrate. People tend to be spaced out with too much alpha and have attention difficulties such as those experienced in ADD and ADHD. Too much alpha can also be a sign of posttraumatic stress disorder (PTSD) and depression, in which an accumulation of chemicals around the nerve synapses clogs the transfer of messages. Meditation can slowly reduce the chemical deposits (they are moved to other locations in the body) so that the emotional charge will let information transmission reoccur.

Lack of alpha activity can be associated with difficulty processing the sensations of taste, hearing, smell, touch, and vision. Without an awareness of your sensations, you can become forgetful, have deadline difficulties, be unable to maintain a schedule, or have increased anxiety and stress. Even with their eyes closed, people with little or no alpha-wave activity cannot become calm. They tend to have memory loss due to the fact that sensation acts as information and is processed into memories and thoughts, which are then stored in the brain and used as a basis of your knowledge. Often these people need a drink of alcohol at the end of the day to reduce their anxiety and get calm. People can become so habituated over time to low alpha that they stop hearing the birds sing or lose the sense of touch. As a result, they forget to pay attention and experience the aliveness of each sensation.

When alpha is deficient, there is not enough mental speed to connect your thoughts and sensations together, and it is difficult to react to information presented to you or to respond to life situations quickly enough. The reason is that the sensory stimuli are not being processed or may even be discarded at the nerve endings. Without enough stimulation, there may be a disturbance in the thalamus, which is the gate or relay bridge for monitoring the amount of sensory information entering the nervous system.

The most important exercises for alpha brain waves are those that increase heart rate and blood flow, such as running, jogging, brisk walking, dancing, aerobics, bicycling, and swimming. You need at least half an hour of aerobic exercise every other day, not only for general health, but also to have an impact on your alpha-wave balance. For example, research indicates that thirty to forty-five minutes of brisk walking has a very positive impact on the body, brain, and one's outlook. I will be giving you a walking meditation that you can incorporate into your daily exercise routine.

As noted, meditation mind training changes the brain structure functions as it reduces the activity of the busy mind. With regular practice, you will notice a difference in your ability to remember things, and you will experience much less mental disturbance. Also, your mind will not be as limited in its perceptions, and you will be able to accept and appreciate other people's experience of the world as well as your own. By working to increase alpha states, you will center your attention on present activities as your mind settles into calmness. On weekends and vacations, you will know how to consciously drop the concerns of the day. In social situations, your centeredness and confidence will make it easier for you to relate to others. You won't need alcohol in order to loosen up and feel comfortable. Your thinking will have a crystal-clear quality, and you will find that you can motivate others when you are in a state of centered awareness.

Alpha Exercises

Your intention in alpha exercises and meditation is to be in the moment by noticing sensations that arise in your inner and outer environment—your breathing, a breeze brushing your face, and so on. You want your observation to be without judgment or analysis. Your attention will be more objective with its focus on the bodily sensations. Alpha is calmer and more detached from the exterior world than beta, which can have an in-your-face quality to it. In alpha, your awareness is on all the sensations that arise in the body, mind, and external world. You are aware of your body and your surroundings but are not judging them in a personal way. You are just being aware of and observing your sensations. Maintaining this objective approach, your alpha brain rhythm will be in balance and you will be centered in the immediate present, not in the past or future. In this state of awareness, you are by definition in the "now."

As your practice deepens during a session, your focus of attention will move from a head-awareness to different parts of your body below your neck. Being conscious of your body brings a relaxed calm. The key objective of alpha exercises and meditation is to calm you down as you close your eyes and become more relaxed. Your brainwave activity slows to produce more alpha waves. When you are relaxed and have a wider inner focus, alpha waves become dominant in the brain and produce a calm and pleasant sensation called "the alpha state." Healthy people produce a lot of alpha activity. The more mind training or meditation you do, the easier it is to produce alpha and the longer you can sustain a continuous alpha rhythm.

Researcher Maxwell Cade noticed two distinct alpha states. The first state was close to the frequency of beta waves. The other state was distinguished by alpha waves that were symmetrical on the Brain Mirror monitor. They were indicative of a passive state in which the person could open their eyes, do mathematical problems, walk around, have emotional experiences, read a book, and contemplate its message. This symmetrical pattern on the Brain Mirror is a state of alpha waves that open the door to what Cade called an awakened mind.

Experiencing Alpha

Here's a simple process to experience alpha. Take a moment to be aware of your body. Notice if there are any tight muscles, aches, or pains. Doing this whole-body scan activates alpha waves. To increase alpha, just close your eyes for a few moments and take several deep slow breaths. Inhale through your nostrils, and then fill your lungs completely. Hold for a moment and then slowly exhale through your mouth. When you open your eyes, simply scan your body again and notice how it feels.

Now do the opposite. To decrease alpha, keep your eyes open and engage in calculated thought like counting backward from twenty to one. Notice the difference between breathing with your eyes closed and with them open while counting backward. If you don't notice any difference, try counting from one hundred back to one.

Enneagram Alpha Affirmations

Here is a set of self-affirming statements for use with the alpha-state exercises. You can use any of the statements as you need them, but there is one statement that applies to your Enneagram type. It is helpful if you say the statement a few times before and after you meditate.

1. **One** (the reformer): Alpha stops my judgments and questions.

2. **Two** (the caregiver): Alpha lets me give myself peace and tranquility.

3. **Three** (the achiever): Alpha lets me find the right pace and rhythm in my life.

4. **Four** (the individualist): Alpha lets me access my imagery and fantasy.

5. **Five** (the investigator): Alpha makes my mind flexible, healthy, and young.

6. **Six** (the loyalist): Alpha reduces my anxiety and fear.

7. **Seven** (the adventurer): Alpha gives me an alert, clear, freedom of mind.

8. **Eight** (the challenger): Alpha brings me a sense of calm and releases anger.

9. **Nine** (the peacemaker): My bodily sensations activate alpha waves.

10. **Any of the types:** Alpha waves increase my neurotransmitter acetylcholine.

There are situations in your life that increase your stress and make it difficult for you to drop into the alpha state. When you find yourself in one, use your Enneagram affirmation as a reminder to stop what you are doing. Close your eyes, breathe slowly, and repeat it at least twenty times. Then just sit for a few minutes observing both external and internal sounds and bodily sensations. This is a basic practice that you can do anywhere, anytime.

Space and Sensations

The intention of this exercise is to experience space and sensations and be able to distinguish between the two. Set a timer for fifteen minutes.

1. Find a comfortable place to sit in a quiet undisturbed environment.

2. With your eyes closed, bring your attention to your breath.

3. Let your breath be relaxed and natural.

4. Allow your thoughts to be quiet. Focus on your breath as it passes in and out of your nostrils. Put your attention at the very tip of your nose and feel the air pass in and out of the nostrils.

5. Put your attention on your thumbs and index fingers. Open them so that they are about two inches apart. Become aware of the dimensions of and sensations in each thumb and finger.

6. Notice the space or empty area around and between both of your thumbs and index fingers. Be aware of the distinctive qualities of the space between your thumbs and fingers, and what the volume of your thumbs and fingers feel like. As you focus on the thumbs and fingers, you may feel them vibrating or tingling.

7. With your next inhalation, notice the air from outside entering your body, filling your lungs and the space of your body with air. Now experience the similar space and air between your thumbs and fingers.

8. Scan your inner body from head to toe, noting this space and the air penetrating every part of your body.

171

9. Open your eyes and be aware of the space between you and any object in front of you. It may be a wall, a tree, or a chair. Put your attention on the space between you and the object, not on the object itself.

10. Notice the sensation and definition of your body (as you did with the thumb and fingers) and the space outside your body.

11. Move your attention back and forth, first with your eyes closed, noticing the space and sensations inside the body, and then with your eyes open, noticing the space outside the body.

12. Journaling:

    •   How would you describe the space between your thumbs and index fingers?

    •   Describe the experience of space between you and the object in the room.

    •   Is there a difference between the experience of space and sensations inside and outside your body?

Walking Meditation

Walking meditation is a model for focusing your awareness on movements and sensations as you move throughout your day. There are many benefits of walking meditation. Like sitting meditation, it balances and centers your mind. Often when you walk, your mind tends to be somewhere else. Walking mediation is a training process in which you give your full attention to each movement made in walking. It is one of the easiest ways to train your mind to focus on doing what you are doing when you are doing it! It is one of the easiest methods of focusing the mind in the here and now.

Walking meditation retrains the mind to become aware of your bodily sensations, which are so familiar that you forget they are even occurring. When that happens, the alpha brain waves diminish the flow of energy throughout the body and brain. Noticing sensory stimuli while you are walking makes it easier to become aware of the more refined sensory stimuli in seated meditation.

Choose a suitable place to walk. Generally this should be a quiet place without much foot traffic so you can maintain your inner focus. At first pick an area about thirty feet in length, either inside or outside. Walk for approximately thirty feet and then turn around and continue to walk back and forth for about twenty minutes.

You will be walking back and forth as you learn to do this meditation. After you are accustomed to the practice, use it on your daily walks. Begin by walking slowly so you can experience the focused sensations. First focus on the movement of your arms and legs moving in a cross-pattern: the right leg and the left arm move forward at the same time, then the left leg and the right arm. As you establish this rhythm, focus individually on each foot as it touches the ground. Notice how the heel touches first and then the rest of the foot. Then the other foot begins to lift the heel and the toe pushes off.

Coordinate your breathing with the movement of your limbs and feet. This type of movement generates electrical activity in the brain that has a harmonizing influence on the whole central nervous system. This is a special benefit from walking that you do not necessarily get from other kinds of exercise.

Pay attention to the feelings and sensations in your feet as you walk. Notice the physical sensations and how they change as you walk. These sensations happen every time we walk, but we tend not to notice such subtle changes. This simple observation increases your awareness as you move through the world. A by-product of this observation practice is a deepening of your curiosity.

As you become familiar with the different sensations from your feet, let these sensations slide into the background of your awareness. After about ten minutes of walking, begin to focus on the sensations of seeing, hearing, and smelling. Take each one of these senses separately, and explore them by focusing more attention on them. Be receptive and open. Don't try to analyze or compare. That is beta activity. Simply deepen the observation process. Notice what your eyes are seeing, your ears are hearing, and your nose is smelling. Allow each sensation to naturally arise as you walk. Without any evaluation, you may first see a tree, then hear a bird song, and then smell the aroma of a flower. Just put your attention on whatever comes into your awareness. All the while, the sensations in your feet serve as a background to all of the other sensations. Next notice how many of these sensations you are able to experience simultaneously. This simultaneous observation takes practice in order for the brain to build new neural networks.

Here is a summary of the steps of walking meditation to make it easier for you to remember:

1. Walk back and forth in a space about thirty feet long for about twenty minutes.

2. As you begin to walk, bring your awareness and attention to your legs and arms.

3. Next place all of your attention on the soles of your feet, and focus on the various sensation and feelings as they come and go.

4. Notice new sensations and feelings as they arise.

5. As you become familiar with the different sensations from your feet, let these sensations slide into the background of your awareness.

6. After about ten minutes, focus on the sensations of seeing, hearing, and smelling, taking each separately. Allow each sensation to naturally arise as you walk. All the while, your feet sensations serve as a background.

7. Next notice how many of these sensations you are able to experience simultaneously.

This is the full sequence, but you may choose not to do all of the steps in the early practice of this meditation. Add steps as you become more able to hold concentration and experience the alpha-state afterglow. I suggest that you practice for twenty minutes a day at least three times a week to begin to experience the walking meditation benefit of increased alpha waves.

Alpha Perception Meditation

For the Alpha Perception Meditation, you will combine the way the brain works with the four prefrontal cortex mind faculties as your tools. Remember the key questions of the faculties: *What is my intention? Where do I put my attention? When am I reflecting? And how am I aware?* Below is a table to help clarify the answers to these questions and give you an idea of what you might encounter in this meditation.

Alpha Perception Meditation: Mind Tools & Guidelines

Intention	Attention	Receptivity/ Awareness
I focus on sensations in my body and in the outer environment (vision, hearing, touch, smell, taste, and feeling).	I place my attention on the sensations of the breath. I focus on the sensations and the space in which they appear. They will be closest in distance to my body as I perceive it in my mind. My breath is not as prominent but will be happening in the background of my mind.	I have a greater sense of being present. I have increased imagery and colors. I have pleasant bodily sensations. I have a sense of lightness, of swaying and rocking. My awareness may alternate between internal and external environments.

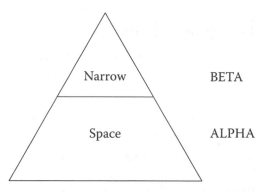

In alpha meditation, your attention moves from a narrow focus on the breath and body muscles (a beta-wave state) to the sensations and the experience of space (an alpha-wave state) in which you perceive internal and external sensations expanding in your awareness.

Preparation

The most important meditation preparation is to be in a place where it is quiet and where you will not be disturbed by the phone, animals, or another person. Find a comfortable chair or meditation pillow to sit on. If seated in a chair, have your feet on the floor. If on a pillow, sit in a cross-legged meditation style on the floor. It is best not to lie down to meditate, as the mind will tend to relax too much, and you will have the tendency to fall asleep.

As you sit, your back and spine need to be straight and your arms loose at your sides. Rest your hands, palms down, on your thighs. As you settle into your sitting position, focus your gaze directly in front of you so that when you close your eyes (or drop your gaze), your head and shoulders will be relaxed. If possible, sit in the same location each time you meditate.

Meditation

As you practice the Alpha Perception Meditation, give yourself enough time to breathe, relax, and let go. If you find you need further direction to relax or want to be guided in this meditation, you can download the CD for it (see appendix). Let us begin.

Alpha Perception Meditation #1:

1. Close your eyes...Be aware of any sounds around you...notice your body in your seated position...make sure you are comfortable so you do not move during the meditation...

2. Use your relaxation marker from the Beta Relaxation Meditation in chapter five to deepen your relaxation. Focus on the image, symbol, or feeling that you chose as your marker of the relaxed state.

3. Let your awareness open to the entire field of tactile sensations... your body, sounds, smell...take three deep breaths...

4. You may notice a visual image of your body. Set that aside and just be aware of the tactile sensations...be aware of what is arising in this field without desire or wanting to make it different...

5. Take a breath...Now focus your attention on the sensation in your nostrils...notice a few more breaths as the air moves in and out of your nostrils...

6. Direct your attention to the crown of your head...focus on a spot about an inch in diameter...let whatever tactile sensations arise at this spot into your awareness...

7. Expand the field to four or five inches on the surface of your head...notice any throbbing...movement...pressure....warmth or cold...tingling...

8. Move your attention to the left side of your head focusing on a four-to-five-inch area...On your inhalation, gradually shift your attention to the right side of your head with a four-to-five-inch focus and notice the sensations as you exhale...

9. Simply notice the senses...there is no adding or subtracting of anything...just focus your awareness on the senses...

10. Gradually, move this awareness up to your forehead...if an image comes to mind, just refocus and be aware of the tactile sensations...

11. Move your attention to your eyes then to your cheeks...nose... mouth...jaw...Expand the awareness to cover your entire face

simultaneously. Note the sensations. Move your awareness from your face to the back of your head by moving through the interior of your head. Notice tactile sensations...Now scan from the back of your head through the interior back to your face, noting tactile sensations...

12. Breathe in, hold for a moment, and move gradually down the neck, noting sensations as you slowly breathe out. With each breath, slowly move down your left shoulder, down to your arm...hand...your five fingers...gently move your attention to the five fingers on your right hand...to your arm...to your right shoulder...

13. Move your awareness to the chest as you breathe in. scan the upper, middle, and lower regions as your breathe out. Shift your attention through the chest cavity, noting sensations in the interior as your attention moves to the back...Bring your attention to the upper...middle...lower back as you breathe in and out slowly...

14. With the in-breath, slide your attention through the interior of your body, noticing sensations in the solar plexus...Slip through the interior and be aware of the sensations in your left buttock... note the different sensations in your two buttocks as you sit on the cushion or chair.

15. Move down from the left buttock to the left thigh then into the calf...left ankle...left foot...into the toes...Direct your attention to the right buttock...thigh...calf...foot...toes...

16. Open and move your focus up to the crown of your head and scan from the top of the head to the bottom of your feet... expand the field of your awareness...simultaneously experience the entire field of tactile sensations in your body... remain in this awareness for a few moments.

17. Now gently bring yourself back to feel where you are sitting or lying. Take several deep breaths. Open your eyes and stretch your body. Before you get up, notice how you feel refreshed

and alert. Continue to feel this state of relaxation moment-to-moment in your daily activities.

18. Journal your experience so that you can observe your development as you go deeper each time you repeat this meditation.

Alpha Perception Meditation #2:

1. Close your eyes...For the next few minutes, settle your body into a comfortable easeful state by relaxing the muscles of your body from head to toe...

2. Use your relaxation marker from the Beta Relaxation Meditation to deepen your relaxation...

3. As your body relaxes, your breath becomes more subtle and noticeable...Take three breaths and on each out-breath let the relaxation go deeper into any tense areas...

4. Let your breath be relaxed and focus your attention on the movement of your belly for several breaths...Now notice the breath as it goes in and out of the nostrils...Notice the tactile sensations as the air passes the opening of the nostrils...

5. When the breath goes out from your nostril, don't send the mind after it. When the breath comes in, don't let the mind follow it. Keep focused at the tip of your nose, the nostril openings.

6. Be the observer as you count the next ten breaths. Start by counting each inhalation until you reach ten. If you lose count, start over at one.

7. Let your attention remain broad and open as your mind stays still like a post at the edge of the sea when the water rises. The post doesn't rise with the water and when the water ebbs the post doesn't sink.

8. Take a moment to notice your sensations...First imagine the sound of a bell using your sense of hearing. Determine where you perceive the sound...Is it in the body or outside of it?...Be aware of the space out of which the sounds arises. Be aware of what happens as the sound fades...

9. Imagine now a visual sensation such as a scene or a color. Are you inside the image or outside of it? Where is it located in your body? Notice where the image arises as well as the shape or texture of the colors...visualize the colors and images with space around them...notice as they fade away...

10. Imagine and become aware of tastes. Where does taste come from...what is the taste of space...and what does it dissolve into?...

11. Imagine any smells. From where does the smell arise...what is the smell of space...and what does it dissolve into?

12. Notice your thoughts. Where are they located in your body...are you inside your thoughts or are they outside your body? Be aware of the space around them...notice where and how they dissolve...

13. Notice any self-talk. Where do those internal voices come from...where are they located in the body...what makes the talk continue...when and where do they dissolve?

14. Notice your thoughts and at the same time notice the felt sense of your body and the space your body occupies—notice your thoughts, your body, and the space simultaneously...

15. Add to your body a sense of now-ness—the sense that you are in the present moment. Experience all your senses—your vision... hearing...taste... smell...felt sense...the space around the body, all simultaneously...

16. Notice as you are aware of all your sensations that the space begins to expand...

17. Take several deep breaths...allow yourself to be in this expanded space for several moments...

18. Now gently bring yourself back to feel where you are sitting or lying. Take several deep breaths. Open your eyes and stretch your body. Before you get up, notice how you feel refreshed and alert. Continue to feel this state of relaxation moment-to-moment in your daily activities.

19. Journal your experience so that you can observe your development as you go deeper each time you repeat this meditation.

Journaling Your Progress

Practice Alpha Perception Meditation daily for a week. After each practice session, answer questions on your progress. You can copy the Alpha Perception Meditation Journal on the next page to use in recording your answers. Only answer the questions that are applicable to your experience in each session.

As we practice the Alpha Perception Meditation, we begin to broaden our narrow fixed view of life and feel more alive. We discover who we are. Bodily sensations are experienced right now, not in the future or in the past. In alpha, we learn to distinguish between analytical abstract thoughts and the physical sensations of our body. When we think in the abstract, we can easily get caught up in the story we create about what is happening to us or to the people around us. But focusing on bodily sensation takes us out of our story into a direct self-awareness of what is actually occurring. Observing ourselves and being aware of our bodily sensations, giving that busy part of our minds a rest, calms us down. With this focus, the parasympathetic nervous system is activated and puts the body-mind into the rest and reset phase. The key point about the alpha state is that we gain access to the observer-self, that inner friend who teaches us how to wake up the conscious mind and conscious brain. Alpha gives us direct access to experience as our questions fall aside and we discover a constant observer in us aware of each moment.

From alpha, we move to the next chapter and into a deeper part of our brain and a slower brain-wave pattern: theta.

Alpha Perception Meditation Journal

Date:

Mental Tools: Intention, Attention, Receptivity, Awareness

Were you aware of your intention when you started? Describe your intention.

Reflect on what thoughts were prominent and how many categories of thoughts were noted? Describe.

Were you aware of your relaxed muscles and what was it like to scan your entire body? Describe.

As you placed your attention on your breath, what sensations did you experience in your body?

Did you experience colors, tactile sensation, sounds, smells, and tastes? Describe.

Were you aware of the sensations being in the body or outside the body?

Were you aware of the difference between the inner and the outer sensations?

As you placed your attention on the inner sensations, describe what the experience for you to be present in your body?

Describe the inner space and the outer space experience?

Describe when the sensations dissolve into the space?

Describe the difference between the solidness of your body and space around your body?

What would it be like to experience this in every day activities? Describe.

Describe the experience of lightness and swaying or rocking.

Recall your intention and how you experience it? And did you have any intuitive insights? Describe.

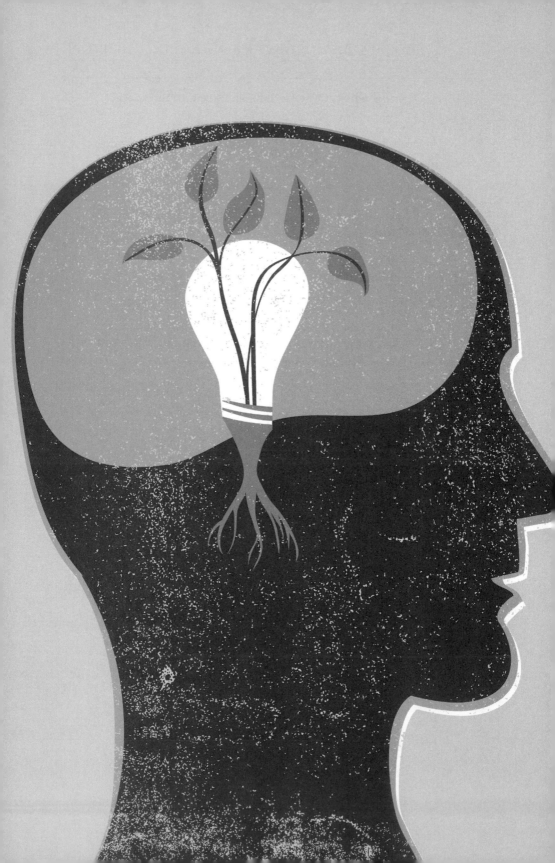

7

Theta Brain Waves and GABA

Emotions cannot be permanent. That's why they are called "emotions"—the word comes from "motion," movement. They move; hence, they are "emotions." From one to another you continually change.

—Osho

During a six-month retreat, my mental concentration became so strongly focused that there was little inward distraction or disturbance. An overarching question I had been asking myself was "What is the nature of reality of this world?" One morning as I became quiet and concentrated, my mind became like a beam of light that both illuminated and shifted my awareness. There were no conscious thoughts. Rather, I was immediately riveted by what I was experiencing. I could not physically move and felt stuck in a profound stillness where everything stopped—no thoughts, no breath, and no sensations. The sudden shift was a perception of the outside world being as close to my face as it could get. It was like a two-dimensional scene plastered against my face. Everything I looked at had no separation or distance from me. In that moment, I realized that the outside world was inside my head. I was making up my world. The startling

185

insight was that I was literally walking around in my mind. From that split second of understanding, I knew that the outside world is a reflection of my inner mind and that there is no separation or no continuum between it and me. This realization wasn't a concept; it was an experience of the truth of the way things are. Through more inquiry, I have continued to receive a broader and deeper perspective about the nature of reality.

When used for discovery and clarity, the mind is a gift you can give to yourself. Learning how to use your theta brain waves is what opens the door to your self-realization. This gift arrives as your mind becomes concentrated and you can receive what you need to know for your transformation.

Imagine yourself in deep reverie, a dreamlike state. In your imagination, you have arrived at a very special vacation destination, a beautiful remote island in the middle of the Pacific Ocean. As you walk along the beach, you hear the waves rolling in over and over again in a soothing chant. The sand is soft and warm as you settle your body down into its inviting embrace, which immediately stabilizes your mind and deepens your attention as you drop all worldly cares. You feel the sand under you and the sun warming your bare body. You smell the sweet fragrance of the sea breeze as it fans your body and feel your relaxation deepening. In this rich moment of your imagination, you become one with your surroundings.

By just reading this description, you may have actually felt that you were lying in the sand, and that your body had begun to relax as you responded to what this imagery invoked in you. Asking you to imagine such scenes using all your senses is what is known as an induction. If you close your eyes and have someone read you this paragraph, your body will probably experience a feeling of relaxation and peacefulness. This kind of induction occurs in the subconscious mind between waking and sleeping, and it is similar to a light relaxed awake-like sleep. This is called a hypnagogic state of mind, and when you are in that state your brain in producing theta waves.

These brain waves are the electrical impulses produced in the limbic system and experienced throughout the body. In our hand model, the limbic system is illustrated by the position of your thumb tucked under your fingers. The "limbic" thumb touches the neocortex, the thalamus, and the reptilian brain (represented by the fingers curled over the thumb). The limbic center is in the middle of the brain and connects to the other parts of the brain. Theta waves link the brain functions from the old reptilian brain to the top of the new brain at the neocortex.

The theta brain rhythm determines how well you handle stress in your life. When the brain waves are erratic, you feel nervous or irritable. And when the brain waves are in rhythmic flow, you are able to drop into the theta state of deep meditation. This is where profound insights arise spontaneously and you feel the urge to create something.

Your learning and emotional life reside in theta waves. Deep hereditary and genetic patterns, as well as family conditioning and that of personal experiences, are stored as memories in the hippocampus of the limbic brain. Many of us carry from early childhood onward the baggage of physical and/or emotional memories of abandonment or abuse.

In regard to confronting negative memories, I am reminded of Julie, an Enneagram 6, who came to see me in order to deepen her meditation practice. In our initial conversation, she talked about how angry she was with her stepfather. She had been verbally abused by him as a young child and felt that trauma was holding her back from a life of success. And despite the work she had done in therapy, she was still stuck. Julie wanted to see the situation in a new way and did not want to define her life around abuse and neglect anymore. While at some level she did not want to face what had happened to her, she knew that she was living a lie by repressing it. Julie was aware that the memory of her childhood abuse had left her feeling unworthy of love or financial success, that she couldn't make it in the world while still feeling this way.

From previous work with other clients with similar histories, I knew that in Julie's limbic memory bank rested a story that fixed her attention and wouldn't let her relax and drop down to access theta where deep meditation and healing are experienced. Rather than starting with a theta meditation practice, we proceeded with an exercise I call Face it, Embrace it, and Erase it. (See the theta exercise section later in the chapter.)

I first had Julie describe her strongest memory of interacting with her stepfather, which was him telling her that she was no good and wouldn't amount to anything. He unmercifully ridiculed the way she dressed, especially when she was wearing jeans, saying she had a terrible figure and should never wear tight pants. (You may recall I referred to this aspect of this client's story early in the book.) To her, the language and tone of his comments had a strong sexual undercurrent. He repeated these disparaging remarks to her many times. She described how she had lost confidence in herself by the time she was a teenager and had a very low self-image.

Using the Face it, Embrace it, and Erase it technique, I had Julie recount the story using all her sensory modalities of touch, smell, color, and so on. For the Erase part of the technique, I had her repeat the story over and over until her sensory responses had totally changed, and there was no longer any underlying emotional charge connected to it. After facing, embracing, and erasing this old story that had held her back in life, we began to create a new story. Toward the end of the session, I took her into a visualization meditation. Afterward she reported seeing an image of herself in a raft that was caught in the rapids but then finally broke free and was brought safely to shore. Julie said that the process left her feeling satisfied, grateful, and with a new level of self-confidence.

To face and then erase old memory patterns is a beginning step. To create a new story provides a new pattern for the brain to connect to and amplify. Changing the function and structure of the brain circuitry takes practice. I gave Julie a twenty-one day practice of "tapping in" her new feelings while imagining the new story we had crafted for her life. This tapping method is called Emotional Freedom Techniques

(EFT; for further information, see www.emofree.com). A wonderful conclusion to Julie's story is that at her next appointment twenty-one days later, she was wearing jeans and had bought three new pairs. At age fifty, it was the first time she had worn them since her teenage years. The combination of the exercise we did and the EFT changed her brain through the practice of neural repatterning and changed her life in the process. A short time later, Julie created a job making money out of a home business and experienced a new level of success in her life.

If we pay attention, these deep buried memories of past wounds stored in the limbic brain generally pop up as an emotional response to some situation in our environment that can hurt others and us. Many people who have been abused either perpetrate that abuse on others or get involved in relationships in which they are abused. In my opinion, the limbic system is the region of the brain that triggers and keeps us addicted to our reactions and resistances, which prevents us from seeing the truth of who we really are. Theta brain waves and their neurotransmitter partner GABA (gamma-aminobutyric acid) hold the key to unlocking the Flow in our body/brain/mind. The key is in knowing how to bring the subconscious into conscious awareness.

Theta brain waves are demonstrated in the full range of emotional responses, which extend all the way from despair to joy. Theta waves are the brain waves of our repressed emotional memories. As I meditated through the years, the top of the reaction scale of emotions became less intense, which was then reflected in my increasing lack of resistance to situations in my life. As the Osho quote that opened this chapter says, emotions are movement. That movement will push away or draw people toward us, but our emotions remain essentially unknown to us unless they rise into conscious intention, focus, and awareness so that we can observe and work with them.

Shining the Light on Painful Memories

After a year of meditation practice, my client Helen, fifty-five, an Enneagram 3, and CEO of a successful company, described the benefits of her meditation "as a way to clarify my mind through self-awareness and to become aware of the world around me as well." When I first began to work with Helen, her alpha and theta waves were very low and she was not conscious of her emotions or her bodily sensations. She would talk feelings but did not really feel them.

At one session, after she had returned from attending a seminar, Helen said that she had met an old friend there, which had triggered a "stashed-away" painful memory from when she was fifteen years old, when her awareness of being in her body got "whacked." As she recounted the story, Helen began to cry. She had stayed overnight at a girlfriend's house with a few other people. She was asleep on the living room couch when she was suddenly awakened by her girlfriend's brother on top of her. She was unable to fight him off and he raped her. All of these years, she had felt guilt and shame about this violation, with pain and tightness in her pelvis. As a consequence, she became emotionally protective and distant from herself and others. She described it as "being alone in a crowd."

As we focused on "unveiling" this tender repressed memory, the brain-wave monitor showed more activity in the alpha brain waves and less in the theta brain waves. I kept having her come back to a feeling of being cared for and emotionally protected. With that, the flow of all the brain waves converged into a pattern of balanced synchrony. After we finished, she said that it seemed like such a simple step to focus on that moment of flow, but from doing it she felt reconnected to a wonderful vibration of energy that moved up and down her body from head to toe. She felt calm, safe, and open to a sense of presence.

In another session, we worked on how to remove her attention from the memory to her tactile sensations of the present. Afterward, she sent an e-mail, saying, "I am flying home today; my heart is filled, my chest expansive, my body relaxed, and my imagination alive with all sorts of possibilities. And yes, Patt, I can feel it right down to my toes!" Today, for the first time in her life and after two failed marriages, Helen is very much in love.

The mind must be aware and conscious enough to see the mechanism that happens in a stress response in order to facilitate a rerouting of that response. We have a choice to change our reaction and that is where the plasticity of the brain comes in to play. What is exciting about working with theta brain waves is that we can reprogram these emotion-patterned memories through awareness and with persistence. I believe this is one of the most magnificent benefits of neuroplasticity. There is a way to clear our past and become present, alive, and fully engaged in life. Our hidden emotional memories are merely "blind spots" for us, because they are accessible to us just below the level of conscious awareness.

We all have these blind spots and simply bringing them into the light of our daily consciousness can transform our lives. The following is an example of the power that comes from shining the light of conscious awareness on to an old memory.

Brent, an Enneagram 7, had just been made president of a new company. I had worked with him for two years and he had become a consistent meditator. He found it a powerful tool in meeting the challenges of leaving a long-standing corporate position and facing the breakup of his marriage. One of his roles as president of this new company was to represent it by regularly speaking in front of the board of directors as well as business groups. When he was hired, the board indicated that they wanted him to take a personal approach in his dealings with them and the employees of the company. In other jobs, he had found it easy to speak in front of groups about business matters, but it had always been difficult for him to talk about himself. He had been embarrassed several times over the years when faced with such situations, and had literally been unable to talk. He would just stand there speechless.

This was Brent's "blind spot." He had no idea what caused it or how to overcome it. In our session, we used the Face it, Embrace it, and Erase it technique. Afterward I got the following note from him: "I wanted to share with you what I'm experiencing from our session. It has left me in a different place. I am able to clearly see an internal conversation that has been running in the background for my entire life. I've had a sense of it, but didn't recognize what was really at work here, and how counterproductive it was for me. What I'm noticing is that the angst attached to the dialogue is gone. It comes up sometimes, but it's occurring more like thoughts in a meditation, they come and they fall aside trusting . . . trusting. Amazing really." He said that there had been only one incident recently when he couldn't find the words. Ever since the session, the brain repatterning worked and for the first time he was comfortable talking about himself in front of groups.

The obvious question from these examples is "What is the purpose for these memories to be hidden?" We all know the answer: to hide our pain. The good news is that underneath the painful memories hides a unique gift for our growth and development as a sane and mature human being. Our life's work is truly to open the doors of this hidden world and reveal these gifts to ourselves.

This can be done with theta brain-wave meditation. In this simple process, you can swing open the gates of the inner mind and delve into your emotional life. Here you can discover a release to express yourself in new and different ways when freed from old emotional patterns and reactions. My own experience and that of clients has taught me that we can meditate our way to freedom.

In 2005, the Research Institute of Physiology at the Russian Academy of Medical Sciences reported the results of a clinical trial to examine how long-term meditation practice can affect EEG activity of subjects viewing emotional and non-emotional or neutral movie clips. This study provided the first empirical proof that meditators are better at regulating the intensity of their emotional arousal and maintaining equilibrium while under emotional stress.

Theta and Intuition

In the theta state, we develop a new bond with ourselves by weaving our emotions together with intention. When we pause to reflect on an intention and recognize the emotion that is connected to it, we create the foundation for a strong internal connection with ourselves. Our inner world contains bodily sensations, emotions, thoughts, memories, beliefs, and perceptions. In investigating my inner world, I forged an intimacy of closeness with myself that I had never known before. This inward-directed intimacy produces a quality of mind that I can rely on; it's always there for me. As I taught myself how to focus inwardly using theta waves, I learned to be in a creative and deeply insightful place that affects every area of my life.

Lauren, an Enneagram 6, is a social worker who was interested in mind training and searching for the right kind of meditation practice for herself when she first came to me as a client. When I viewed her brain-wave pattern, she had high beta waves and inconsistent theta waves. The Braverman neurotransmitter assessment revealed that she had a dopamine deficiency. She became anxious easily and used caffeine and chocolate to keep her going during the day. She had all the hallmarks of GABA dominance, including great social skills and concern for others. As a type six Enneagram personality, she always needs to know the answer to questions in order to clarify her thinking mind. After several sessions of teaching her different meditation tools, her practice became strong and consistent, and she was able to stabilize her anxiety and inquire into the theta state for personal answers to many of her life questions. She told me that practicing my Theta Wisdom Meditation CD (see appendix) trained her to relax, not get attached to her thoughts, and expand her mind. She commented that this state was a deep, quiet, dark, and "floaty" place and that the meditation/brain work was a miracle for her. It taught her not only how to get very quiet, a blessing in itself, but also how to get answers to questions that were intuitively inspired.

One of her work-related conflicts was whether to leave social work and start a counseling practice or be part of the family business. When she asked the question while in theta, the answer came clearly that it was to have a counseling practice. The insight was so powerful that she has never doubted or regretted the answer. This is a big test for this Enneagram type because doubt is one of their key challenges. She now loves her work. Lauren says, "This process has given me confidence and self-empowerment. I would dread doing some things because I would have to 'think' of how to do them. I can now relax into theta and ask 'how' or 'what' and the answers come. This has made my life easier and more exciting. The future is more colorful and creative for me. The wonder is that I don't have to rely on just my thinking mind. I have the confidence to try new ideas and faith to know they're possible. Meditation has been a gift to me."

Developing the mind to use theta state also works in relationship with another person. When you take the time to become open to another's emotional intention, you create an interpersonal connection. Being in touch with your own emotions enables you to sense another's. This mutual emotional awareness brings you closer to the other person and to yourself. In this shared moment, you feel "felt" by that person. This is the heart of human intimacy and the kind that we all want. Intention is the link to the moment of our actions and reactions. Sharing those mental states is the underlying experience to linking up with yourself and others. Let's begin to explore how to access theta in order to open this hidden door of power and potential within us.

The brain functions in such an intuitive way that when your intention is to shift into the theta level of mind, you can just focus your attention deep inside yourself to your belly, back near the spinal cord, and this signals the limbic brain that you are willing to let go of external awareness. As you deepen down to the theta level and your attention becomes unfocused, the mind moves into the space inside the body. As this mind shift occurs, the body's boundaries may appear to dissolve as the inner space of the body and the outer space of your surroundings become one and the same space. Robert Adams, one of my teachers, would say that theta is when you are the pot (your body), and when the clay pot cracks, the air on the inside of the pot mingles with the air on the outside. It is in this theta mind-state that the central nervous system reduces input from the peripheral nervous system, which normally serves to protect it from sensory overload caused by stress or physical damage. The lowering of sensory input into the brain reduces neural control, and paradoxically the brain expands its functioning powers. The normally unused portion of the brain becomes active and performs at maximum capacity. Knowing how to move one's mind into theta opens this capacity.

GABA

The limbic system produces the neurotransmitter GABA. Its role is to supply the brain with a check-and-balance system. GABA acts similarly to the brakes in a car. Its function is to keep the car running neither too fast nor too slow. As with brakes, GABA has an inhibitory function, which keeps all the other neurochemicals in check and operating at a steady pace. GABA inhibits the informational flow when you overextend your emotional nurturing tendencies, in other words, maximize your GABA nature. But it also inhibits the informational flow when you feel hurt at not having your own needs met .GABA contributes to the constancy, frequency, and amplitude of the beta and alpha waves. When GABA is deficient, the emotions and anxiety run wild and are uncontrollable. When this happens, the Flow closes its prefrontal lobe regulation with GABA, which is directly involved in how you handle stress. The beta and theta waves cannot connect when the mind is locked in a negative loop of anxiety and/or irritability. In the stress response, the overuse and depletion of GABA, resulting in the loss of its braking effect, allows addictive emotions to take over. On the other hand, the brakes can be so tight with an overabundance of GABA that you can have a severe emotional reaction to something that would normally not upset you.

In theta meditation, you will notice your mind becoming more stable, soft, and calm. These are the effects of GABA. This neurotransmitter is also involved in the production of endorphins that produce what is known as the "runners high," a feeling of calm and some would even say euphoria. Like GABA, hallucinogens (LSD, DMT, psilocybin mushrooms, peyote, etc.) promote the theta state; I don't recommend achieving theta that way.

To keep GABA in balance, include these foods in your diet: almonds, walnuts, bananas, oranges, grapefruit, spinach, broccoli, potatoes, lentils, beef liver, halibut, oats, rice bran, brown rice, and whole grains. When theta is working correctly with GABA, you are levelheaded, your emotions are available, your inner organization runs smoothly, and you have a focused and straightforward approach to the issues you face daily.

Too Much or Too Little

When you have too much theta and too much GABA, you can be overly nurturing and giving to people in the extreme. In fact, you can exaggerate your emotional response to others. With too much theta, emotions are strong and constantly running your behavior and interactions with the world. When GABA is flooding your system, it is difficult to hold back any emotion you are feeling. For example, if you thrive on giving of yourself in organizations in order to be recognized and loved, you may have a strong emotional reaction when the recognition is not forthcoming. This behavioral pattern of wanting to serve to receive is debilitating to any positive emotional state. Old patterns like these are the source of an excessive buildup of brain waves and chemicals that create what I call addictive emotional patterns.

The brain waves are not running smoothly when the brain is not producing enough GABA. Sometimes the electrical output of the waves is generated in erratic bursts called brain arrhythmia, and feelings of emotional well-being drop to a low level as a result. Theta can influence beta-wave output when not in its steady rhythm, affecting the rhythm of your heart as will as increasing muscular pain and stomach disorders. When theta is out of rhythm, it also affects alpha and can produce attention deficit, memory lapses, or mild hysteria like laughing and crying inappropriately. There is an overriding edge of emotion such as anger or fear. When in the theta state, your brain cells reset their sodium-potassium ratio. After an extended period in the beta state, the ratio between potassium and sodium can be out of balance, causing mental fatigue. A brief period in theta (5–15 minutes) can restore the ratio to normal and result in mental refreshment.

Theta Exercises

Enneagram Theta Affirmations

Here is a set of affirmations you can use while working with the theta exercises. You can use any of the statements as you need them, but there is one statement that applies to your Enneagram type. Saying the statement a few times before and after you meditate can facilitate transformation.

1. **One** (the reformer): Theta is a new way to see myself and the world perfectly.

2. **Two** (the caregiver): In theta I can feel cared for and supported.

3. **Three** (the achiever): Theta lets me be my true self.

4. **Four** (the individualist): Theta is where my creativity nudges me.

5. **Five** (the investigator): In theta I explore my early beliefs and life experiences.

6. **Six** (the loyalist): Theta is my emotional healing center and everyday refuge.

7. **Seven** (the adventurer): Theta creates freedom and an even, calm pace in my life.

8. **Eight** (the challenger): Theta changes my stress and emotional responses.

9. **Nine** (the peacemaker): Theta changes my emotional-mental-behavioral patterns.

10. **Any type:**

    • In theta my brain's plasticity is used to change my beliefs, traumas, and the past memories that do not serve me.

    • Theta is where I can make clear and definitive decisions.

    • Theta is the place of universal insights and my personal intuition.

- In theta I become stable and calm without me having to change the chaotic outside world.

- In theta my brain waves activate and balance the neurotransmitter GABA.

Belief-Behavior-Emotion Exercise

The key feature of theta is to decode your personality with its beliefs, behaviors, and attitudes. These personality characteristics are learned, programmed, and stored in the limbic system and function with theta brain waves. Through imitation as children in our early "holding" environment, we acquire personality characteristics from our parents and others. This transference happens at a very early stage of development, and then we incorporate these beliefs at an older age. Unconsciously, working from the theta level of awareness, our beliefs and personality behaviors trap us very quickly into a narrow sense of self.

Following are the basic beliefs, behaviors, and emotions of the Enneagram personality styles. The first list is about the self-defeating beliefs that have been handed down to you, stored in memory, and are now held in your subconscious mind. The second list is basic personality behaviors and the third is the emotional fears. If you don't already know your type, you may recognize yourself in these patterns.

Beliefs Associated with Enneagram Types

1. **One:** I am not accepted as I am. I can't make mistakes. I am a mistake. If you knew who I was inside me, you wouldn't want to be with me.

2. **Two:** I must give love to get love. I must be needed. I will help you no matter the cost to me. I can't have my own needs.

3. **Three:** I am an independent doer. I am rewarded for what I do, not for who I am. I must create an image of myself to look good.

4. **Four:** Something is missing in me. I am flawed. I am addicted to emotional ups and downs. I want to hide inside myself because it is not okay to be happy.

5. **Five:** The world demands too much of me and gives me too little. Withdrawal is the safest place for me.

6. **Six:** I don't trust the world or myself because it is a threatening and dangerous place. I constantly doubt myself about everything.

7. **Seven:** The world is a limiting place. I can't depend on others. The world is frustrating and causes me pain. Keeping active and making plans keeps the pain away from me.

8. **Eight:** The world is unjust. The powerful take advantage of the innocent. Being angry and aggressive protects me from being vulnerable.

9. **Nine:** I am unimportant and I will blend in with my environment to feel comfort and belong. It is not okay to be aggressive or assert myself.

Behaviors Associated with Enneagram Types

1. **One:** I am a good responsible person. I suppress my anger. My job is to fix and correct everything.

2. **Two:** I need to be needed and I live for others. What I feel they need I am ready to provide.

3. **Three:** I seek affirmation and achievement. I don't know how to express my true feelings or values.

4. **Four:** I search for love. I strive to be an individualist and to be loved through my uniqueness and individuality.

5. **Five:** I am a private, self-sufficient individual. I accumulate knowledge, limit my desires, and tend to be miserly.

6. **Six:** I am fearful, questioning, and vigilant for security.

7. **Seven:** I desire pleasurable activities. I am a glutton for new ideas and possibilities.

8. **Eight:** I blame others and proclaim myself blame free.

9. **Nine:** I forget my self, merge with others, and devalue my priorities.

Emotions Associated with Enneagram Types

Fear is an emotion that can run your beliefs and behaviors, and set your attitudes. Fear was programmed into you in infancy. When you release the emotional programming that drives these beliefs and behaviors, you realize your essential nature. In your behaviors, you can see both your beliefs and emotions. Your emotions put your behavior into motion. Releasing these behaviors through conscious access to theta, where they are stored, moves you naturally into your core essential nature.

1. **One:** Judgmental of self and others. Releasing being judgmental of self and others moves me to serenity.

2. **Two:** Pride. Releasing being prideful moves me to kindness.

3. **Three:** Feeling rejected and like a failure. Releasing feeling rejected and like a failure moves me to love and bliss.

4. **Four:** Feeling disconnected. Releasing feeling disconnected moves me to joy.

5. **Five:** Feeling overwhelmed. Releasing feeling overwhelmed moves me to peace.

6. **Six:** Feeling abandoned. Releasing feeling abandoned moves me to stillness.

7. **Seven:** Feeling deprived. Releasing feeling deprived moves me to inclusion and deep connection.

8. **Eight:** Feeling confronted. Releasing feeling confronted moves me to my strength.

9. **Nine:** Feeling separated. Releasing feeling separated moves me to connection and peace.

If you've determined your Enneagram type, pick the three statements representing your type in each of the categories and write them at the top of a sheet of paper. If you have not determined your type, choose the statement in each category with which you most identify.

For example, for me as an Enneagram 6, my three statements are:

Belief: I don't trust the world or myself because it is a threatening and dangerous place. I constantly doubt myself about everything.

Behavior: I am fearful, questioning, and vigilant for security.

Emotion: Releasing feeling abandoned moves me to expansiveness.

After you've written your statements, follow these steps:

1. For the belief statement, reflect back to some place in your childhood and up to your age, and write three examples that describe your experience of that belief.

2. For the behavior statement, choose three concrete experiences and write about how that behavior played out in your life.

3. For the emotion statement, notice it has two parts. The first is where the emotion of fear is hidden in the behavior. For me my fear is hidden in abandonment. The second is the release from the fear of abandonment into the core positive nature of my Enneagram type. From the emotion statement, describe how your fear created your behavioral response. For me, it was how my fear created abandonment in my life. Then describe what it would be like if you were completely free and released into your essence, as in my case, to the nature of vast emptiness and spaciousness.

When we consciously own and then release our belief, behavior, and emotional patterns, we open up the flow of our natural energies. When release happens, the neural pathways get reactivated and strengthened and connected back to our essential personality core. Immediate changes in our behavior are experienced naturally in our everyday life.

Naming Your Feelings

The intention of this exercise is to diminish emotional responses by disrupting the brain activity in the limbic region and producing brain activity in the prefrontal cortex. Recent research has found that putting feelings into language and labeling the emotion can activate the prefrontal cortex and dampen the responses from the limbic region. This helps to alleviate emotional distress and reaction. I have found that when I feel anxious, I immediately notice where the anxiety is in my body and say to myself, "I am anxious but I am safe. " I notice a reduction in intensity and a fading away of the emotion.

This exercise can be done with eyes open or closed. Whenever you experience a distressing emotion, just label what you are feeling. You need not analyze it or judge it, just label it exactly as it occurs. This will switch the activity from one part of the brain to another and reduce the emotional response. Write down your distressing emotion and give it a label. For example: "I feel very upset about Phil's comment that I can't do the job." The emotion is anger and fear that it might be true. The label, as it continues to come to mind, is "anger and fear." When the thought about Phil's comment arises, label it "anger and fear."

Merging into Space

The intention of this exercise is to use meditation to shift pain, emotional responses, and negative events by how and where you place your attention and awareness.

1. Allow yourself to relax using your marker (image, symbol, or feeling) from the Beta Relaxation Meditation.

2. Become aware of your sensations of hearing, touch, smell, seeing, feelings, and thoughts and the space in which they arise as in the Alpha Perception Meditation.

3. Take several deep breaths, allow your mind to begin to travel downward, and focus your attention in your heart. Observe your mind going deep inside, with a downward and backward movement. Rest your attention between your heart and your spinal cord. If you are conscious of the rhythm of your heartbeat, allow your breath to move with your heart rhythm. You are now deeply relaxed but still aware of your position in the chair

or on the meditation pillow, as well as the space in which the sensations arise inside your body.

4. Now become aware of the sensations in your two thumbs and the amount of sensations that are in and fill your thumbs. Notice the felt sense of the space surrounding each thumb, and notice the difference between your thumbs and the space that surrounds them. (Note: your thumbs may feel tingly, solid, and have a circumference with fullness. The space in comparison may not have a circumference but an open, soft, free, and unbound sense.)

5. Experience each of your other fingers—index, middle finger, ring finger, and little finger—in the same manner.

6. Inhale deeply, and as you do, notice the unbound air space as it dissolves with the air space inside your body. As you breathe out, your inner air space merges with the outer air space. Continue breathing a few more times, until the boundaries of your body begin to dissolve and the inner and outer space continually merge. There is now a soft intimacy and closeness, and a sense of being held in space unbounded, in a restful expansive unity. Relax deeply in this restful state.

7. Remain present and aware of what occurs in your expanded restful mind. Gently and effortlessly without conscious direction, observe your mind as it moves from sensation to sensation. There may be a pain in your body. If that occurs, rest your attention on the pain and then notice its location, size, and sensation. Become conscious of the space in which the pain resides; this is similar to how you experienced the space surrounding your thumbs. As you breathe out, let your attention move away from the pain. As you breathe in, move your mind closer to the pain. Each time you breathe out, experience the breath and space dissolve. This allows the pain to melt into space or dissolve away. As you breathe the outside space within you and breathe the inner space out of you, both inner and outer spaces merge with

the pain and become one with the dissolving pain. (If you are aware of your heartbeat, try to breathe in that rhythm.)

8. Notice the essence, the new kernel of feeling that results from this inner and outer joining process. The essence may be a sense of kindness, impermanence, tenderness, softness, serenity, love, energy, openness, compassion, gratitude, emptiness, happiness, and/or freedom or purity.

9. You may also experience a destructive emotion or memory, or a past event as well as a physical pain. These emotions may be fear, anxiety, anger, and grief. Practice the same melting process for these negative experiences.

10. Once you complete the exercise, move your attention back into ordinary consciousness. Journal your experience. What was the essence of yourself that you touched and experienced?

11. Each time you meditate, experience the essence hidden behind any physical or emotional pain that may arise.

12. Practice this felt sense of essence again and again so it becomes embedded in your neuronal pathways. Doing this practice will evolve your neuroplastic brain into positive mental qualities that replace the habitual destructive mental states that we all contend with every day.

Face It, Embrace It, and Erase It Exercise

What would it be like to have your automatic emotional and behavioral responses erased from your life? The Face It, Embrace It, and Erase It exercise enables you to do this whenever they occur. In this exercise, you will explore the emotional memories stored in your limbic region. These are repressed memories that still affect your behaviors and trigger destructive and disturbing emotional reactions. These behaviors are conditional imprints, genetically encoded patterns, and painful experiences tucked far away within your subconscious so you won't feel or remember their origins. Although deeply buried, they are still retained as a chemical imprint in your memory. Whenever a stimulus comes along that matches the original emotional experience, this memory gets triggered and you fall into behaving in the same way, driven by this old pattern. You relive those emotional memories over and over again throughout your life as the imprint gets repeatedly activated.

Many of us have gone through a lot of talk therapy to release the disturbance from deep emotional trauma. Others, like me, have sat in meditation for long hours. As the anxiety or pain naturally arises out of the depths, I've tried to honor it without judgment and then keep my fine focus on the pain of the trauma to dissolve into the pain. Both of these techniques have helped many of us heal the deep emotional wounds we carry.

In this exercise, we go a step further and follow the pathway to the imprint where the emotional memory is stored. Once the characteristics of the pathway are established, we reverse the direction. With this method, the way in which the brain has encoded the thoughts are unraveled in the *opposite* direction from how they were originally processed.

I discovered this process unexpectedly when my husband was in a near-fatal accident. It happened a few years ago when he and his son were hiking along a river trail. Unfortunately, he decided to swim across the river when the current was swift and very cold from the snow-melted water that had been released from a reservoir into the river that day. As he started to swim to the other side of the river to his son who had already swum across, the current whisked him away downstream. In the tumbling rapids, he was thrown about and banged up against the rocks. The coldness of the water lowered his body temperature to a dangerous level. He rapidly moved into hypothermia; all his blood rushed to his core organs, and as a result his arms and legs began to go numb and feel like lead weights. He attempted to reach the bank several times, but his low energy left him weak and he was swept down a series of rapids into the spin of a whirlpool. He was sucked underwater and struggled to the surface. His son had been scrambling over large boulders along the river to get to his father. As his dad was about to be pulled under by the whirlpool again, he dove into the water and pulled his father to the riverbank. Once there, my husband lay in emotional shock, his body bruised and his spine injured.

In the days that followed his rescue, my husband awoke at night with extreme pain in his body at the spots where the rocks had hit his back. He would try to stretch his body to reduce the pain, but the pain did not subside. One evening, I was studying about the brain and the way it encodes emotional memories. I had also been reading a book by Francine Shapiro, a psychologist who developed the therapeutic technique Eye Movement Desensitization and Reprocessing (EMDR). For this, the client is asked to visually track a pencil or other object as the therapist moves it back and forth in front of the client. The client's lateral eye movements unlock disturbing memories. This therapy is very effective with acute stress disorder and posttraumatic stress disorder. The American Psychiatric Association 2004 Practice Guidelines as well as the U.S. Department of Defense highly recommend this therapy for the treatment of trauma disorders. Spontaneously, I put the two ideas together and decided to see if I could relieve my husband's pain by actually having him relive his near-death ordeal via the brain sequence protocol and EMDR.

We sat in the big chairs in our living room and, while using the EMDR technique, I had him repeat his experience of being swept down the river and almost drowning several times until he felt an emotional distance from the traumatic event. Through the Face It, Embrace It, and Erase It process, my husband remembered his thought at the time: "Am I going to live or am I going to die?" The more he felt the body sensations from the pounding of water and rocks against him and facing the fear by confronting the situation objectively over and over again, the fear and the thought-imprint began to dissolve. Embracing this fear became pivotal to his body healing. The fear-thought was trapped in his bodily sensations in the hard, sharp pain from the pounding of water and rocks against him. From the underlying agitation of terror, it formed an unconscious mantra running deep in his subconscious mind: "Am I going to live or am I going to die?" As we repeatedly reviewed the events on the river and the sensations that accompanied them, this terror became objective, as if it were someone else's horror story. At the end of the process, my husband breathed a deep sigh of relief and felt serenity for the first time since the accident. He slept through that night without pain.

For all of us who are carrying trauma, there is a buried sense of serenity in us, the gift beneath a trauma. A good question to ask yourself is: "What is it that I am unwilling to give up to reveal this felt essence of who I truly am?"

Here are the specifics steps of the Face It, Embrace It, and Erase It emotional release process that you can use for yourself.

1. **Face It** (This recreates the outer structure of the situation.)

    • Recall a past traumatic event or difficult situation in your life (a difficult encounter with a person, an old memory that surfaces, a past event recently revealed through a triggering circumstance, or any other stimulus). Identify the initial cause of the incident, as well as past occurrences and any parallels or connections in your past or present history.

    • Write about the situation in as much detail as you can.

2. **Embrace it** (This creates the internal structure of the situation.)

    • Close your eyes

    • Describe the memory of the event or circumstances in terms of your behavior and how it presently is affecting you.

    • Describe the emotion(s) stimulated.

    • Open your eyes and write down the emotion(s).

    • Close your eyes again and find the location in your body where this emotion resides.

        o   In what part of your body is the emotion located?

        o   What is the size of this emotion? Describe it in inches.

        o   What color is it? Does it have a smell or taste?

        o   What is the texture of the emotion? (rough, smooth, prickly, wet, dry, soft, hard, etc.)

        o   What is the temperature of it? (hot, cold, etc.)

o   Write down your sensations.

- What is the thought that conceptualizes the situation? (a belief, idea, principle, conviction, etc.)

- Write down the your thoughts.

3. **Erase it** (This releases the personal story to an objective memory and a transformational essence.)

- On an arbitrary measure of 0–10, how intensely are you absorbed in your story right now?

- Read out loud the external and the internal structure of the memory as you wrote them in the previous two steps.

- As you tell the story of the event, with all its sensory properties, move your index finger rapidly back and forth in front of your face, across your line of vision, and follow it with your eyes. The finger moves horizontally back and forth from the extreme right to the extreme left of your visual field. The distance the hand travels on each sweep should be at least twelve inches. There should be two movements back and forth per second; each back and forth eye movement is counted as one movement. This practice desensitizes and disrupts the neuronal pathways that hold your repressed emotional memory. The focused attention of the eyes following the finger movements disrupts the sensations and begins to objectify the story, When you have finished telling the story once through, stop the finger movements.

Check and Repeat

1. Take several deep breaths with your eyes closed.

2. Recall the external and internal structure of the memory.

3. Has anything changed in your mental or emotional feelings? Do you have any new thought or have any new memories arisen? If so, write them down.

4. Once again, measure the intensity of the memory you are experiencing on the 0–10 scale. Write it down.

5. Repeat the previous four steps until the measure of the intensity of the circumstances has little or no emotional reaction for you.

6. When your story has a low intensity on the scale, notice what you are now feeling. (For example, there may be a sense of freedom, love, purity, energy, compassion, caring, emptiness, well-being, kindness, serenity, etc.). Write it down.

7. For the next two weeks, every day when you meditate, feel the emotional shift and transformation you felt. As you meditate, feel the merging and dissolving into this new felt sense of yourself called essence. This will allow a synchrony of neuronal pathways to be established and a neuroplastic change in your brain toward happiness.

Theta Wisdom Meditation

For Theta Wisdom Meditation, you will combine the way the brain works with the four prefrontal cortex mind faculties as your tools. Remember the key questions of the faculties: *What is my intention? Where do I put my attention? When am I receptive? And how am I aware?* On the next page is a table to help clarify the answers to these questions and give you an idea of what you might encounter in this meditation.

Theta Wisdom Meditation: Mind Tools & Guidelines

Intention	Attention	Receptivity/ Awareness
To attain knowledge and experience. To be directed toward inner self.	Attention is expanded, broadened, and extended. Movement is dropping downward. Location of attention is in the back of the body. Movement is stabilizing.	Detached, alert, and settled. Floating feeling. Lucid clarity and satisfaction. Vagueness and darkness. Sensation of numb limbs. Loss of body boundaries. Expansive dissolving. Lightness or heaviness. Vivid heartbeat. Feeling soft, intimate gratefulness.

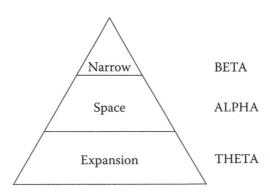

Your attention has moved from a narrow focus on the breath and body muscles (beta) to the sensations of the space in which sensations arise (alpha). Your attention is now on theta where inner and outer space merge.

Sound Meditation

A few years ago I was traveling back from India. When we changed planes in Japan, I met the eyes of a beautiful Indian man who was dressed as a Sikh. He smiled and I smiled back. When we landed in Los Angeles, we came off the plane at the same time and waited together to pick up our luggage before going through customs. I began to talk with him and found out that he had come to work with his students in the Sikh community in the United States. He introduced himself and told me that he was a master of Nada yoga, which is the practice of sound as a means of attaining enlightenment. Since I have always loved to sing, I was extremely interested in finding out more about this practice. After meeting in the airport, we communicated by e-mail. On his next trip to the United States, I invited him to come to my meditation cottage and teach me sound meditation. This is an ancient practice with complicated rhythm patterns that one learns to chant. I found the experience and practice with him exciting and it touched me deeply. The following exercise is a simple version of how to experience a sound that can take you to theta, to a deeper, more expansive place within.

1. Find a comfortable sitting position with your back straight and your chin on a parallel with the floor.

2. Relax your body, and using one of the meditation exercises we've worked with, clear your thoughts for at least ten minutes and become aware of the sounds in the surrounding environment and the sensation of hearing them. This could be birds singing, dog barking, and people's voices.

3. Notice your breath as well as the rhythm of the inhalation and exhalation of each breath. Practice this inward focus for a few minutes.

4. In theta, you want to develop the ability to watch consciousness in the form of the breath. Now notice the gap between the breaths. Move your awareness into this gap between breaths with your observation on what is occurring there.

5. Make the sound *AH* and keep repeating, one *AH* after another. Place your awareness in the gap of space before you hear your *AH* sound. The gap is the space immediately before the sound arises and after it falls away. Keep your attention there in the space as consciousness carries the sound on the breath.

6. Your eyes are now focused inward, into the gap of space. You will notice that your gaze is both in and out at the same time, but your attention is to be focused inward.

7. It is suggested that you make the *AH* sound for only 20–30 minutes in one sitting.

8. Keep a daily journal of your experiences and insights. Use the writing as a way to ground the steps in your shift of conscious awareness.

Inquiry Meditation

Inquiry into your inner world is one of the keys to gaining access to theta. The use of inquiry or consciously asking yourself questions breaks open your subconscious mindset. The limbic system is connected to the cortex, and theta brain waves interact closely with the beta waves. Inquiry uses both of these brain waves together as a way of receiving and executing the answers to questions you ask yourself. I have taught the following technique to executives in order to help them make better decisions for their organizations, to artists to be more creative, and to housewives to solve family problems.

1. Before you begin to meditate, formulate a question for which you want an answer.

2. Close your eyes and move into a deep relaxation. Follow the steps to go in, back, and down into the theta brain-wave frequency. As you put your intention inward, notice your attention moving back almost to your spinal cord, and then just let your mind fall and drop down gently. As you settle into this grounded state of mind, be patient with yourself. You are exploring new mental territory and theta has its own way of teaching you how to travel in it.

3. Without effort and by not using your linear thinking mind, the answer to your question will arise in the form of a symbol, image, word, or a felt knowing.

4. When something arises in your mind, open your eyes and write it down. Close your eyes and go back down as many times as needed to get the answer. It is important to record your answers or you will forget them.

5. When you complete the meditation, use the beta mind to put your answer into a concept, to make plans, or to execute the plan.

Your mind is always ready to respond to the intention of inquiry and to your search. The answer is always there at any time. Inquiry can also be used as contemplation on life itself, such as asking the questions: Who am I? What is life? What is real? What brings meaning to me? What is time? What is space? Exploring these questions opens wisdom, meaning, and depth in your life.

People say that Einstein did his work in theta. Cats are in theta much of the time. Just watch them as they are stalking. They will hold the same position, not moving, for long periods of time. Yet, they are both relaxed and alert, watching from the theta part of their brain. Theta is the dreamlike state that holds your creative, intuitive, inspirational, and emotional information. If your inspirations do not become conscious, they will not come to fruition in the world. Inquire regularly into this amazing world you hold inside of you.

Theta Wisdom Meditation

Preparation

The most important meditation preparation is to be in a place where it is quiet and where you will not be disturbed by the phone, animals, or another person. Find a comfortable chair or meditation pillow to sit on. If seated in a chair, have your feet on the floor. If on a pillow, sit in a cross-legged meditation style on the floor. It is best not to lie down to meditate, as the mind will tend to relax too much, and you will have the tendency to fall asleep.

As you sit, your back and spine need to be straight and your arms loose at your sides. Rest your hands, palms down, on your thighs. As you settle into your sitting position, focus your gaze directly in front of you so that when you close your eyes (or drop your gaze), your head and shoulders will be relaxed. If possible, sit in the same location each time you meditate.

As you practice Theta Wisdom Meditation, give yourself enough time to breathe, relax, and let go. If you find you need further direction to relax or want to be guided in this meditation, you can download the CD for it (see appendix). Let us begin.

Theta Wisdom Meditation #1:

1. Close your eyes...For the next few moments settle your body in a comfortable easeful state by relaxing the muscles from head to toe...

2. Use your relaxation marker from the Beta Relaxation Meditation to deepen your relaxation...

3. As your body relaxes, your breath becomes more noticeable. Take three breaths and on the out-breath, relax any tense areas...

4. Let your breath be relaxed and focused on the movement of your belly. As the breath goes in and out of the nostrils, notice tactile sensations at the nostril opening from your inhalation and exhalation...

5. Place your attention deep inside your body...Let your attention be in back and near your spinal cord...Observe the rhythm of your breath as it automatically moves in and out at your belly...

6. Let your mind begin to move downward, relaxing like a falling leaf in space...softly downward...The air and space on the outside of the body and the space and air inside your body begin to join...the outside air mixes with the inside air...allowing boundaries to dissolve...gently...as the movement of the breath flows easily...moving naturally back...and forth...merging together...as you move downward...

7. You are moving deeper in this space where there is a softness and warmth...

8. Now visualize yourself gently moving down a stairway...it feels as though you are being gently directed down...easefully...

9. You continue to flow down the stairs until you get to the bottom...At the bottom of the stairs there is a corridor; continue along this corridor...There is light and there are twists and turns...You move under archways, through circular doorways... and then the corridor angles slightly downward...

10. You are moving toward an inner world that holds a flow of events...of memories...of new possibilities...a journey to your home base of well-being...healing...meaning...

11. As you come around the last turn in the corridor, you begin to see movement...lights...sounds...a magnificent place is beckoning you...

12. In front of you is a bridge. It crosses a mote to a magnificent heart-shaped mansion...In a few moments, you are going into this house. First, observe the front door and note what it may say on it...As you open the door and enter the house, you observe that it is actually configured like a heart with four chambers or rooms. The main floor has two chambers and there is a winding stairway down to two other chambers.

13. Now move down the hall to the door on your right. There is a sign on the door that reads "The Chamber of Wounds." When you open the door, notice what is in this room...in this space...check carefully...you can change anything you want...in a few moments we are going to leave the room...finish making changes...As you leave, you know that you can go back at any time.

14. Now go across the hall to the second room on the left. The sign on the door reads "The Chamber of Healing." When you open the door, notice what is in this room...in this space...check carefully...you can change anything you want...in a few moments

we are going to leave the room...finish making changes...As you leave, you know that you can go back at any time.

15. Now go down the stairway to the lower chambers...you go down into a lighted hallway. There is a door on your left labeled "The Chamber of Creative Insights." When you open the door, notice what is in this room...in this space...check carefully...you can change anything you want...in a few moments we are going to leave the room...finish making changes. As you leave, you know you can go back at any time...

16. Go across the hall to the last room on your right, to the door labeled "The Chamber of Decisions." When you open the door, notice what is in this room...in this space...check carefully...you can change anything you want...in a few moments we are going to leave the room...finish making changes. As you leave, you know you can go back at any time...

17. As you come up the stairway, pause outside the door of the Heart Mansion. Notice what you have to be grateful for from your experience in this magnificent mansion...Know you can always return to receive more wisdom and clarity.

18. Now gently bring yourself back to feel where you are sitting or lying. Take several deep breaths. Open your eyes and stretch your body. Before you get up, notice how you feel refreshed and alert. Continue to feel this state of relaxation moment-to-moment in your daily activities.

19. Journal your experience so that you can observe your development as you go deeper each time you repeat this meditation.

Theta Wisdom Meditation #2:

1. Close your eyes...For the next few minutes settle your body in a comfortable easeful state by relaxing the muscles of your body. Let tension drain from your face...shoulders...down to your toes...

2. Use your relaxation marker from the Beta Relaxation Meditation to deepen your relaxation...

3. Let your breath be relaxed...Focus on the movement of your belly...on the breath as it goes in and out of the nostrils... Notice the tactile sensations of temperature, pressure, and movement...

4. Observe the entire field of tactile sensations, noting especially the body's solidity...the movement of the belly...and the breath tactile sensations...Notice any tingling in the body...

5. Let your body relax more as you soften your belly...take three slow deep breaths and on the out-breath let go of any tension... at each breath, release any deeper tense areas of the body...

6. Observe your breath as you relinquish all effort and control of it...allow the breath to be natural as it moves in and out automatically. You will notice even a deeper relaxation.

7. Allow the breath as you breathe in and out to join with the field of space and air from the outside and inside your body, to blend, open, and merge into a more relaxed and expanded space...

8. Now as you rest your mind back into this expanded soft warm space, feel a gentle movement downward as if an escalator is gently sliding you downward...softly...slowly...gently...

9. As you continue to move downward, let yourself drop deeper and deeper into this smooth...quiet...yielding...healing place... Feel the relief and appreciation of being totally held...

10. Open your eyes slightly in an unfocused gaze. Gaze into the field as at a blank TV screen....let your awareness relax in the space in front of you...

11. It may take a few moments before thoughts...desires... memories...images...emotions begin...but in time they will arise. As they arise, say, "This is the Mind's space."

12. Observe your thoughts without reacting...judging...labeling... without any attempt to control...just let them be...be present with them...

13. Notice from where the thoughts come...and where they go.

14. If you get caught up in thought, relax more deeply and return to the space of the mind. The idea is not to get rid of a thought, but just to let go of holding on to the thought. If you get spaced out or have a wandering mind, generate an image to bring yourself back…Soon the mind's movement will slow into stillness…

15. Continue practicing for a few moments…

16. Now gently bring yourself back to feel where you are sitting or lying. Take several deep breaths. Open your eyes and stretch your body. Before you get up, notice how you feel refreshed and alert. Continue to feel this state of relaxation moment-to-moment in your daily activities.

17. Journal your experience so that you can observe your development as you go deeper each time you repeat this meditation.

Journaling Your Progress

Practice Theta Wisdom Meditation daily for a week. After each practice session, answer questions on your progress in quieting the mind and relaxing your body. You can copy the Theta Wisdom Meditation Journal to use in recording your answers. Only answer the questions that are applicable to your experience in each session.

Theta Wisdom Meditation Journal

Date:

Mental Tools: Intention, Attention, Receptivity, Awareness

Describe your relaxation process.

Indicate prominent thoughts. Which thoughts did you attach to and which were dissolved?

Indicate sensations experienced. Which ones were prominent?

Describe the breath and where it was placed: belly, lungs, or nostril.

Were you able to observe the breath and be detached without giving it direction? Describe the experience.

Describe the experience of oneness, of moving through the boundary of your body.

Describe the expansiveness, lightness, or heaviness.

Indicate the process as the movement of going down, back, and in.

Describe the mind as it became stable, soft, and grateful.

What were the insights that were revealed to your question?

Describe your inner world while in the theta state.

The key to mind-training is that you do have choices and are responsible for your emotions because they are your emotions. To blame others for your feelings is to keep emotional trauma alive. Blaming and projecting your pain onto others only repeats the same pattern over and over again in new circumstances. Being willing to accept responsibility for your emotional life brings the reward of self-respect. And this opens the door to self-love and all the grace and forgiveness that emanates from love.

There is a gift that comes from every story. After the destructive emotion disappears with the help of the mind-training tools presented here, the healing emotions closer to your true essence appear. These are compassion, love, forgiveness, emptiness, kindness, caring, energy, intuition, energy, and beauty. Each takes the place of the destructive emotion. At a conference, I heard the Dalai Lama say, "A destructive emotion is like a coin that has been buried in the ground and when removed, the coin is still covered with dirt. Once cleaned off, the sparkle of the bright metal appears which was there all the time." There is a sparkle, under the painful repressed emotions, that is always there within us.

Remember the story of the ancient sailors who took with them on their sailing trips a "land-finding crow." When gales blew the ship off its course and they were cast adrift with no land in sight, they released the crow to search for land in all directions. If it spotted land, it would fly straight in that direction and guide the ship to safety. If it didn't sight land, it returned to its perch on the masthead ready to be sent out again. You have an inner crow, an inner guidance system that will lead you "home." Once your emotional load is lightened and you have found the essence of peace within, you will have discovered your own home base. You will find then that you are less reactive to the spectrum of emotional provocations. Your mind no longer needs to attract emotional situations that can cause it to lose its connection to your inner home of peace. The mental tools you have developed will help you maintain this stability on the next stage of your journey: the slow delta brain waves in the reptilian brain.

8

Delta Brain Waves and Serotonin

Most people are asleep. They live asleep, marry asleep, breed children in their sleep, and die in their sleep without ever waking up, never understanding the loveliness of existence.

—Anthony de Mello

The person that suggested we go out into the night and look into the sky was an amateur astronomer. He told us this was a particularly good night to observe because the atmosphere was so pristine clear. The night was warm and we all laid down on the grass, looking up into the heavens. As we looked up at the night sky, I could feel myself along with others around me becoming totally absorbed in the vastness and never-ending scope of the Universe. My gaze did not focus on any one thing and I was without evaluation or concern about what we were observing. The sky began to suck me into its vastness. In this state, my awareness was fixed in the sensory moment of stargazing. I could sense in the stillness and my own slowness of breath that we were all totally absorbed.

Even though we were a group of ten people, in this other absorbed state of focus, no personal selves existed. On this dark hilltop, each self was detached from the normal world and its inter-actions and concerns. Our minds were bereft of thoughts, and what remained was a state of just pure being. Finally, someone said, "Oh, a shooting star," and as we all turned to look, the amazing moment of oneness was gone, as each of us again became an evaluator and judge of the world and ourselves.

Most of us have had these kinds of moments in our lives. They come spontaneously, we love them, but we don't know how to get back to that wonderful state of pure beingness and unself-consciousness. The experience of lying in the grass watching the night sky and being fully absorbed into it was an experience of the delta brain-wave state.

Delta is the last of our brain waves to be explored. In delta, the electrical frequency is very slow, and this rhythm affects us much dif-ferently than the other brain waves. The contrast is dramatic between the consciousness of delta and the consciousnesses of beta with its narrow focus and its analyzing intensity. With delta, there is a recep-tivity that includes everything. In the delta state, the mind is quiet of intrusive thoughts. In delta, you are held in total support by some source beyond the mental human world. This state comes when the mind's awareness is aware of itself. It is rubbing noses with itself, so to speak. This state of being aware of one's awareness sparks an incred-ible peace that is beyond belief. It is a happiness that is deep and all-encompassing.

In *Stop Sleep Walking Through Life!* author and researcher Devdas Menon describes this state: "Due to the rapid pace of our lives, it leaves little time to slow down enough to move into the delta brain waves. This quiet state is the primitiveness that we have evolved and is connected to all of nature. Thinking and reasoning are a hindrance to evolving into this dimension of mind that allows the mind to awaken. One must break through to this slow-paced movement and be in accord with the nature of its depths that exists in the universal intel-ligence. Awakening implies discovery of this dimension."

Delta is expressed in the reptilian brain. In the hand model of the brain, the reptilian brain is in the palm of your hand. If you recall from part I, this brain is the oldest brain and deals with sleep and the automatic body functions such as heartbeat, blood flow, small muscle movements, and the fight-or-flight response.

Delta is the unconscious level of mind that holds the deepest quality of who we are, an inner stillness, a reverie of no self, the awareness of what actually exists. If you were a car, you would now be in overdrive. The brain waves are slow, and so we are very quiet and very deep but openly focused and integrating the "letting be" state. When in this deep state and also in sleep, we reintegrate information to be categorized and stored in memory.

Researcher Bruce O'Hara from the University of Kentucky found that when subjects meditated before they went to sleep, they improved their sleep patterns. After meditation, he found the subjects dropped easily into delta brain waves during sleep. Two-thirds of sleep time is in the delta state and it is needed to complete repairs in the body and to give the brain time to rest. The research indicated that meditation restores the brain and that meditators may require less sleep. If sleep is the home of the delta state, what is it like to be in delta in waking life?

Ben, age fifty, president of a division in a high-tech company in Silicon Valley, had all the trappings of financial success and lived a life others could only imagine. He is an Enneagram 9 who forgets himself in order to stay connected to people. Because of his affable nature, his staff adores him and he inspires his team to produce incredible creative work. His colleagues appreciate and revere him. But a few years ago, Ben felt the need for an inner connection and began a search for personal meaning. He joined a spiritual community, but it did not quench his thirst for inner union. A mutual friend referred him to me.

When I reviewed his waking brain-wave pattern, he had high activity in delta waves and the assessment showed he was deficient in the neurotransmitter serotonin. When a neurotransmitter is deficient, there may be health issues or imbalances. Ben indicated in the interview that he had recently gained weight, felt vulnerable, drank too much alcohol, and had intimacy issues. His second marriage was on the verge of falling apart. He shared that his sleep was often interrupted with bad dreams that revealed a fear of being trapped, which is how he felt about his marriage, but he didn't leave because of his fear of being alone. He dreaded walking into a dark home with no one there.

When I monitored his brain waves, something extraordinary happened. With his eyes closed, I took him through my normal evaluation protocol. Periodically, amplitude explosions appeared in all the brain waves at once. I could not tell whether he was grimacing or crying when this happened. After the session, we reviewed what he had experienced. Ben said that when he closed his eyes, he saw himself in military duty in the first Iraq war. I questioned him further and he started to cry, and then told me something he had never told anyone. He had been in Special Forces, and his job had been to torture Iraqi soldiers for information.

Ben sobbed from the guilt and shame he had held since then. He was living in a PTSD state with repressed emotional pain. I listened to the complete story, and then we did the Face it, Embrace it, and Erase it exercise. He released the story and moved the guilt to forgiveness for his actions. He knew he had been out of his truth and integrity. After the experience, he felt a connection to his heart for the first time in years. He had yearned for this release for so long. We worked on the practical structure of his life situation, and I gave him my Beta Relaxation Meditation CD (see appendix) to begin his meditation practice. I suggested he continue the work at repatterning his brain with a therapist skilled at working with PTSD. Soon after, he moved out of his home and ended his marriage. He is now living in an apartment and dating. His yearning for inner connection, which led him to meditation and mind practice, will continue to heal and rewire his brain.

As meditation deepens there is a point where the mind is only aware of its own awareness. Some say this is the area of the brain where consciousness is fed. The Flow, as described earlier, begins in the brain stem and then moves to the neocortex that touches and connects the mind to all levels of the brain. Through its mental faculties, all levels of the brain resonate into relaxation of thoughts and muscles, the awareness of sensation, the stabilizing of emotions, and the connection to our deepest core of stillness. As this resonance happens, there is an increase of neural networks firing in tandem and in synchrony. Through this process, the mind integrates and awakens to a universal state of awareness of itself.

Research has shown that when all the brain waves are in synchrony, your attitude is consistently positive. Synchrony is what integrates the neural pathways. When you are in stress, your emotional responses stop the Flow. The following is an example of a person with cancer who faced the need to maintain a positive attitude for her healing.

Laura, an Enneagram 9, is a therapist who teaches anger management in prisons. When she came to me, she had recently completed an intensive treatment for Hodgkin's disease. She was thrilled to find a mind-training process that would aid her in healing from the disease. Laura liked learning about the different brain waves and what to expect from each brain structure. She said, "Each of the brain structures and their brain waves enabled me to find pathways in my mind for different kinds of healings." After radiation treatments, she became concerned about her lack of sleep. She would wake up in the middle of the night and could not get back to sleep. "Sleep is essential for my healing," she said. "Before I learned about mind training, I used to get up and read a book for hours because my mind would become increasingly negative if I stayed in bed and tried to fall back to sleep."

We found that Laura was deficient in serotonin. I encouraged her to practice the Delta Synchrony Meditation and listen to the CD (see appendix) to aid in her healing. As she practiced with the breath and the pregnant pause of awareness, she expanded into the deep delta consciousness of stillness. She described her experience: "I first dropped into an alpha-theta state of consciousness with its wonderful visions and insights. By the time I became aware of being awareness in an expansive state, the next thing I knew I would wake up and it was morning. The deep sleep of the slow delta waves was essential to heal both my mind and body."

There is an Indian fable that tells of a guru and his son sitting beneath a banyan tree. Uddalaka, the guru, questions Svetaketu, his son: "How did this huge tree come into existence?"

The young man replies readily, "It came from the seed."

"But," asks the guru, "how did the seed come into being?"

The young man does not have an answer for that question. So the guru asks him to pick a fruit from the tree, break it open, and take out a seed. Svetaketu does what he was asked. Then the guru asks Svetaketu to break open the seed and look inside. There is, of course, nothing inside the seed. The son says, "But there is nothing inside."

The guru responds with a final question, "Has the huge tree grown out of nothing?"

This is the question for the delta level of mind. Delta opens us to the state of nothingness. It is the vastness about which all the spiritual teachers from every tradition speak. In this level of mind, we are in the pregnant pause of nothing, the space between waves, the breaths, and the space between heartbeats. In my own story, when I said I fell into "the gap," this is the same level of consciousness as the pregnant pause of nothing or vast space. It was as if I fell through a gap in consciousness into the vastness all around and inside of us. I came to call this place "home base."

After one of my meditation circles, a young man named Win, an Enneagram 7, shared with me his experiences doing the Delta Synchrony Meditation. He described experiencing the expansiveness of just being still and touching some vastness, of being aware of himself being aware—of his surroundings, his body, and his alert, vital mind free of personality bias. He told me that when the gong sounded while he sat in the meditation circle, Win immediately felt his energy, or his mind (he didn't know how to name it), expand outward beyond his body. This expansion felt like waves that continued to ripple outward from within him, moving into a blissful infinity. As the sound of the gong dissipated into softer and softer sound waves, the vibration seemed to penetrate deep inside him. He felt a loss of boundaries and seemed to fall into a peaceful place of calm and centeredness. This "no place" was like an automatic movement of breath with an inhalation and exhalation going back and forth.

At one point in his experience, he became aware of an unconscious decision to align with and move forward on his path. There was another startling moment when a strong release of anger, sadness, and grief occurred. After this explosion, he felt a great relief. As he sat in this growing peacefulness, he found himself floating in space, aware of everything, including the birds singing outside the room and the presence of everyone in the circle. He said, "My brain was awake while the body was so calm and at rest. There was a connection with everyone and everything." Win touched that place of liberation and freedom. He experienced the freedom of his self shifting into that immense quality of beingness.

Touching that place is the journey we are all on, whether we realize it or not. Until a baby is two years old, the primary brain wave is delta, which reflects growth happening from the inside out and the fact that the child is sleeping most of the time. Most of us lose conscious access to delta after this initial period of development. But some retain a natural connection to it. Hands-on healers, for example, have an abundance of delta brain waves. They are naturally quiet and deep, and when they are in alignment, all their channels are open to assist the mind and body to heal others. These people are able to put themselves "in the other's shoes," while not losing their own self. This is the quality of a healthy delta person—one who does not get lost in another's emotional story but feels what they are feeling and is able to extend love and energy to them. Buddha called this person a bodhisattva, the compassionate one who aids others in reaching their highest state of development.

Delta can take us to a higher state of awareness than most of us generally experience. Awareness of awareness is a reflection or reflective activity of the mind. It is at a deeper level where there are no words, concepts, or self-observation. At the same time, it is an automatic mind-map of knowing what occurs before we have conceptual understanding.

Serotonin

Serotonin helps the brain's networks move into a harmonic time-and-rate rhythm called synchrony, which simply means a simultaneous occurrence of neurons in different parts of the brain firing at once. Serotonin allows the neural pathways to open in tandem. The flow of the brain functions and neurotransmitters move without resistance, and it permits neuroplastic changes to happen in the brain's prefrontal lobe as it touches each area of mind in unity, in aliveness, and in centeredness. In this rhythmic movement, there is no reaction or resistance; the body is in complete homeostasis, and there is no experience of suffering. Serotonin aids the other brain waves to recharge and rebalance as well.

People with healthy serotonin levels are realists responsive to sensory experiences and love to participate in activities. They like getting things done immediately, and they develop through making changes in their lives. Via delta brain waves, serotonin helps regulate the basic life functions such as the heartbeat, respiration, and sleep. It can also make a person hypervigilant. Serotonin helps maintain routines that require cognitive processing and precise timing of finger movements as in writing or playing a musical instrument. People dominant in this neurotransmitter are not deterred by setbacks or struggles. They are generally optimistic, cheerful, and easygoing. When serotonin is in a healthy chemical mix, the body is in peak performance. Everything is in balance and there is no resistance or reaction to anything. Serotonin is also needed in order to sleep deeply, for food to taste good, and for serenity and satisfaction. Serotonin is essential for the mind to be awake and fulfilled.

High levels of serotonin and plentiful delta brain waves indicate the profile of someone into deep introspection and attracted to prayer, meditation, yoga, or chanting and a regular aerobic exercise program. Li Po, the Chinese philosopher says, "The birds have vanished into the sky, and now the last clouds fade away. We sit together, the mountain and I, until the mountain remains." This, Li Po says, is when the automatic, habitual thoughts and memories of the ego self dissolve. It is the delta state that can dissolve them. Once dissolved, with the burden of the self gone, there is lightness and joy. Uncontrollable thoughts no longer enslave us, and as thought subsides, there is an awareness of the innate natural rhythms of life.

In this rhythm, you wake up in the morning aware of the birds singing and the sun streaming through the window, adding to your curiosity of the new day's unfolding. You are aware of splashing water on your face, feeling it tingle your skin. Then on your morning walk, you notice the light on the trees, the breeze on your face, and your feet touching the ground at each step. Gratitude for nature's providence spirals though your entire being. As the walk continues, there is a point when the walking begins to walk itself. You are not doing it; it is doing you. The physical awareness of delta brain-wave patterns allows the walking to just walk, talking to just talk, and hearing to just hear.

The synchronistic rhythm of life moves in and through us, and we become aware of it as the brain waves slow. Wisdom comes to us when we discover the vastness, immensity, and stillness in the depth of the ocean of our minds. We then have the ability to deal with the all the ripples of discomfort on the surface with calm assurance knowing that the ripples are not the totality of our existence. At this level, we are perfect instruments in the same way as a beautiful harp is perfect when its strings are tuned. When our brains are properly tuned, we begin to harmonize with the Universal music. We are open to the natural flow of beingness. And just as the musician must blend his instrumental voice with the orchestra, we must blend with the Universal flow while remaining human.

In the synchrony meditation, we are in the unconscious mind but conscious of it. There is no personality and no body. It is a place of being that is awakened in the reptilian brain. The more we allow the brain-mind this level of awareness, the more the Flow is an automatic conscious state for us. As Jesus said, this state is like "being in the world but not of it." Each of us, in our own way, desires this freedom, this liberation from the pain and struggle with our chattering minds, and wants to step into this "being" state. Through the ages, teachers from all traditions have described this process as possible for anyone.

All of these teachers and traditions have described how our minds can be transformed and become a virtual paradise.

Too Much or Too Little

Your sense of psychological well-being can be disturbed, however, when the electrical delta volume is turned up too high and too much serotonin is secreted. When this natural flow of delta and serotonin is upset, nervousness and anxiety become a hypervigilant radar system. You begin to check out everything. You are on your toes looking out for your own survival. Your sensitivity increases, especially to criticism and what others think of you. Criticism is a major issue as you become critical of others as well as yourself. You may become so absorbed in checking out what other people are thinking or saying about you that you lose your self-identity. The boundaries between you and others overlap so much that it is unclear who is who, and who's saying what. You become fragile and oversensitive from this lack of boundaries and with no inner direction of your own.

You are also out of synchrony with too low a volume of delta waves and too little serotonin. You may feel too tired to sleep or too drowsy most of the time. You may find it difficult to focus enough to get tasks done. Also, there may be sleep issues such as falling to sleep on the job or going to sleep at night, and then waking up frequently and having difficulty getting back to sleep. Low delta and serotonin also contribute to uncontrollable food cravings, which may result in overeating and obesity.

Delta brain waves increase the neurotransmitter serotonin. The foods that help replenish serotonin deficiency are high-protein foods and avocado, cheese, chicken, chocolate, cottage cheese, duck eggs, granola, turkey, whole milk, and yogurt.

Enneagram Liberation Qualities

The liberation qualities of the Enneagram types offer a picture of delta-serotonin balance. The quality of liberation shines through for that type when the individual is not attached or caught in the dramatic reactions of negative automatic thoughts. Whatever your primary type, with which of the following qualities do you resonate in your life at this time? You will feel like a harp playing a perfectly tuned note.

1. **One** is the reformer; the liberation quality is to be wise.

2. **Two** is the caregiver; the liberation quality is to love unconditionally.

3. **Three** is the achiever; the liberation quality is to be genuine.

4. **Four** is the individualist; the liberation quality is to be self-renewing.

5. **Five** is the investigator; the liberation quality is to be pioneering.

6. **Six** is the loyalist; the liberation quality is to be an inner authority.

7. **Seven** is the adventurer; the liberation quality is to be satisfied.

8. **Eight** is the challenger; the liberation quality is to be heroic.

9. **Nine** is the peacemaker; the liberation quality is to be self-remembering.

To be in liberation is like being a post half-buried in the sand at the edge of the sea. As the sea rises, the post doesn't rise but stays strong and firmly in place. You have the stability and security of a post when you claim your true essence, the true nature of your personality. Finding its truth in you brings the feeling of finally coming home from a long journey.

Delta Exercises

Enneagram Delta Affirmations

Here is a set of affirmations you can use while working with the delta exercises. You can use any of the affirmations as you need them, and especially before and after the Delta Synchrony Meditation, but there is one statement that applies to your Enneagram type.

1. **One** (the reformer): In delta I am in a quiet mind state. There is a stillness and serenity that recharges and renews my body and mind.

2. **Two** (the caregiver): My healing abilities are centered in delta.

3. **Three** (the achiever): In peak performance situations, I am in delta synchrony.

4. **Four** (the individualist): Healing and creativity come in delta synchrony.

5. **Five** (the investigator): Delta is the being state of an alive insightful mind.

6. **Six** (the loyalist): Delta lets me rest in total security and peace.

7. **Seven** (the adventurer): The space between words, breaths, and heartbeats is a pregnant pause that opens me to the synchrony of my being.

8. **Eight** (the challenger): Delta lets me be totally loved by others.

9. **Nine** (the peacemaker): Stillness and great peace is in the depth of my being.

The Clock

The intention of this exercise is to balance your energy to prepare you for the Delta Synchrony Meditation. This is a method one of my teachers taught me to move into the slow brain waves of delta and keep the mind alert and awake.

1. Find a comfortable position and a quiet undisturbed place. Close your eyes.

2. Relax your muscles and notice, without attachment, your mind's chatter.

3. Be aware of the inner tension and tactile sensations in your body and let them dissolve.

4. Imagine a clock (the kind of clock with hands) placed at the base of your spine and the time is 12 o'clock.

5. Observe your breath and its natural rhythm for a few minutes.

6. With the next inhalation, start the breath as you move your focus from visualizing 12 o'clock up to your pelvis; exhale as you put your attention back on the clock.

7. With your next inhalation, place your attention on 12:15 and then move your attention to your belly; exhale, going back to your clock.

8. With your next inhalation, place your attention on 12:30 and then move your attention to your heart; exhale and move back to your clock.

9. With your next inhalation, place your attention on 12:45 and then move your attention to your throat; exhale and move your focus back to your clock.

10. With your next inhalation, place your attention on 1:00 and then move your attention to your forehead; exhale and move back to your clock.

11. Do three rounds from 12:00 to 1:00.

12. In the fourth round, inhale from 1:00 on the clock at the base of your spine to eight inches above your head. Repeat three times.

Seven Breaths

Pranayama is the fourth "limb" of the eight limbs of the Raja yoga system in the Hindu tradition. *Prana* means "life force, vital energy, or breath." *Ayama* means "to lengthen." Pranayama is the yoga of breath control that increases the energy and vitality of our body and mind. There are many breath-control exercises, and students are cautioned about the power pranayama can create in the body and its impact on the psyche. Pranayama is done as a prelude to concentration and meditation practices. The Seven Breath practice is a good one to energize you in preparation for mediation, or if in meditation you become sleepy. The principle of the practice is to breathe and hold the breath for seven counts.

1. In a sitting posture with back straight, inhale several deep breaths through the nostrils and out through the mouth. This is to clear the lungs of stale air.

2. Begin a slow inhalation to the count of seven. Stop and hold the inhalation for a count of seven.

3. Exhale slowly for a count of seven. Stop and hold the exhalation.

4. Inhale again to the count of seven. Stop and hold the inhalation.

5. Repeat this complete cycle of inhale, hold, exhale, hold, and inhale for seven times.

6. When you finish the seven cycles, release the last inhalation, take several deep breaths through the nostrils, breathing out through the mouth, then settle into your exercise or meditation practice.

Delta Synchrony Meditation

For Delta Synchrony Meditation, you will combine the way the brain works with the four prefrontal cortex mind faculties as your tools. Remember the key questions of the faculties: What is my intention? Where do I put my attention? When am I reflecting? And how am I aware? Below is a table to help clarify the answers to these questions and give you an idea of what you might encounter in this meditation.

Delta Synchrony Meditation: Mind Tools & Guidelines

Intention	Attention	Receptivity/ Awareness
To attain knowledge and experience. To be directed toward inner self.	Attention is expanded, broadened, and extended. Movement is dropping downward. Location of attention is in the back of the body. Movement is stabilizing.	Experience of an essence of attunement. Sense of no self. Awareness of the awareness. Surrounded in light. Reduced body awareness. All is well and complete. Nothing matters, just to be. Knowledge of the Universe.

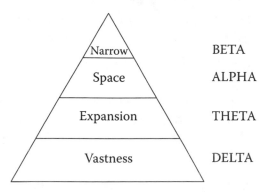

Your attention has moved from a narrow focus on the breath and body muscles (beta) to the sensations of the space in which sensations arise (alpha). Your attention is where inner and outer space merge (theta). Now your attention is in the center of the vastness where vastness is all there is and you are that.

Preparation

The most important meditation preparation is to be in a place where it is quiet and where you will not be disturbed by the phone, animals, or another person. Find a comfortable chair or meditation pillow to sit on. If seated in a chair, have your feet on the floor. If on a pillow, sit in a cross-legged meditation style on the floor. It is best not to lie down to meditate, as the mind will tend to relax too much, and you will have the tendency to fall asleep.

As you sit, your back and spine need to be straight and your arms loose at your sides. Rest your hands, palms down, on your thighs. As you settle into your sitting position, focus your gaze directly in front of you so that when you close your eyes (or drop your gaze), your head and shoulders will be relaxed. If possible, sit in the same location each time you meditate.

Meditation

As you practice the Delta Synchrony Meditation, give yourself enough time to breathe, relax, and let go. If you find you need further direction to relax or want to be guided in this meditation, you can download the CD for it (see appendix). Let us begin.

1. Close your eyes...Scan your environment for sounds...feel the space of the place you are in...notice the positioning of your body as it occupies its space...Feel comfortable and safe...Relax your eyes...release the outer focus of your eyes...expand and open your forehead...Open to the space in your body...relax any tense areas...soften your body...let your arms...legs...buttocks drop into a solid relaxed heaviness...The body is in a state of deep relaxation...

2. Use your relaxation marker from the Beta Relaxation Meditation to deepen your relaxation...

3. Be aware of the rhythm of your belly...your breath moving in and out...Imagine with each exhalation a deeper relaxation release...soften even more...allowing the breath to slow...

4. Observe your breath...notice the tactile sensations in the nostrils. Notice in your nostrils any tingling...movement...pressure... heat or cold...Breathe in and out seven times, counting each inhalation.

5. Be aware of the pause between the inhalation and exhalation...it is like the pause between heartbeats...notice the space within the pause...

6. Notice the space inside your body from the top of your head down to your heart...Allow your mind to drop back and down into space at your heart...As you begin to move down, visualize a dark and silent staircase that descends into your inner refuge...Move downward...the body space expands...becomes transparent...penetrating the walls of your body...inviting these boundaries to open...gently...naturally...

7. As you move down, your body softens...let go even more... an openness emerges between the inside and outside of your body...it keeps expanding even more...

8. Drop into that grounded place of your refuge, into your sanctuary...Your awareness is like the space of your body—soft, relaxed, yet alert and vibrant.

9. Open your eyes just slightly...gently gaze into the space in front of you, not looking at any objects...The sensation is almost like daydreaming...Notice in the foreground of your mind any thoughts taking place...

10. Observe without reaction or feeling distracted whatever emotions, memories, or thoughts arise...As you simply observe these states, your mind begins to settle...

11. In the empty space, you will notice there is something else going on in the background...that is your awareness of the space... Withdraw your attention from thoughts, sensations, and mental activities...Draw your awareness inward and turn your attention on it and observe its own nature...

12. To maintain the balance of this awareness, use your in-breath to turn your awareness inward, then release with the out-breath any thought or mental activities into space...shift your attention from foreground to the background of your awareness with each breath...

13. Notice what is controlling your awareness...What is this nature that is turning inward and releasing these thoughts?

14. Rest your awareness within your own nature...simply be aware of ongoing awareness...sensation of sound and thoughts will arise but don't direct your attention to them.... just have interest in awareness itself...

15. Now release the focus of the breath but sustain the awareness in the center of your consciousness—not inward or outward, just resting in the center, in its own awareness as you stay in the center. Imagine or hear a bell (you can use an actual bell or gong here) as it rings open your mind like a bouquet of flowers being untied...falling open 360 degrees, in all directions, releasing all tension, any holding of yourself. Release yourself into the vastness, into the energy reharmonizing all levels of your being...letting the brain and mind move into synchrony...this is a return to your natural state...you are free...

16. Rest in this natural state of freedom for several moments...

17. Now gently bring yourself back to feel where you are sitting or lying. Take several deep breaths. Open your eyes and stretch your body. Before you get up, notice how you feel refreshed and alert. Continue to feel this state of relaxation moment-to-moment in your daily activities.

18. Journal your experience so that you can observe your development as you go deeper each time you repeat this meditation.

Journaling Your Progress

Practice Delta Synchrony Meditation daily for a week. After each practice session, answer questions on your progress in quieting the mind and relaxing your body. You can copy the Delta Synchrony Meditation Journal to use in recording your answers. Only answer the questions that are applicable to your experience in each session.

The primary purpose of delta brain waves and their chemical partner serotonin is to put us into deep sleep and to wake us up. Sleep is a time to regenerate the mind, brain, and body and to place the day's events into memory. At the heart of delta is the experience not just of sleep, but also of deep, timeless stillness. Delta is the entrance into the vast experience of infinity and space. When the trained, stable mind stays alert and remains conscious in the delta brain pattern, it too can become aware of the awareness of its own stillness. As you master the ability to drop into this deep conscious state in the reptilian brain, you will be absorbed into the vastness of inner space where there is no personality, bodily sensations, or thoughts. There is only a wide-open sense of beingness unequaled to anything you can conceptualize with your neocortex and its beta brain waves.

This level of consciousness brings a vivid, clear, awakened compassion that is open and receptive to everyone and everything. Periodically, we all drop into this liberated state at the moment when all four brain waves move into synchronicity and merge in the Flow. A continual awakening to this reality opens you to a direct experience and knowing of the truth of reality as it actually is. This state is the true beginning of real wisdom. This is a universal quality of mind that is not self-serving but serves both you and others. When deeply in the

---

Delta Synchrony Meditation Journal

Date:

Mental Tools: Intention, Attention, Receptivity, Awareness

Describe being in the pregnant pause.

What is it to be aware of your awareness?

When you are choiceless, what happens when the flow moves without interruption?

What essence arose? Who are you?

What Universal truth was revealed to you?

What is completeness and well-being?

How will you bring this consciously into your everyday life?

Describe vastness.

---

delta state, your self-centered quality vanishes along with the personality self. What remains is a liberated quality of conscious beingness that lives and breathes through your body and mind. Living in this state, you experience a completeness of our life and a reverence for all things as you continually deepen and stabilize into Life's stillness.

As more and more people experience these deeper states of mind and rewire their brain circuits and chemistry, we are collectively evolving the brain of the human species and manifesting in our behavior a state of kindness, love, and caring for our planet. The simple mental practices that we can do every day are the steps on this evolutionary path. The mind-brain is facile, flexible, and plastic. With training, such as the tools provided in this book, it is possible to reprogram what blocks its Flow and move quite rapidly from a less evolved state of mind to a higher state, one that better serves us and the life around us. What we learn is that we can choose to evolve and create a conscious mind as well as a conscious brain.

If you look closely at nature—from the bugs, birds, animals, and fish to the grass, sky, trees, and humans—you find a clear resonance to all life that is the doorway to delta. As you come to experience the quiet moments of delta, you may discover an amazing spacious depth as forms appear and disappear and a powerful inner stillness remains. In this state you discover the extraordinary in the ordinary as the mind and brain become consciousness.

Afterword

A human being is a part of the whole, called by us "Universe," a part limited in time and space. He experiences himself ... as something separated from the rest, a kind of optical delusion of his consciousness. This delusion is a kind of prison for us, restricting us to our personal desires and to affection for a few persons nearest to us. Our tasks must be to free ourselves from this prison by widening our circle of compassion to embrace all living creatures and the whole of nature in its beauty.

—Albert Einstein

At the beginning of this book, I described facilitating a hospice grief group and how the man who had lost his wife started me thinking about how far away most of us are from the center we search for in our lives. As I noted, this became a primary motivation for me to write this book: to let others know that it is possible to find home base, that inner refuge from stress and suffering.

In the period that I was leading grief groups, the Brain Mirror electroencephalograph appeared in my life. I realized as I learned to use the Brain Mirror that this instrument could be a valuable means to train people to adapt to other mental environments than the ones that trap them. Research has demonstrated that we have multiple levels of brain frequencies; unfortunately, many of us are unconscious of their existence. To take refuge from the beta state of our fast-paced, hectic culture is sorely needed today. But more important, I wanted to show people that there are other levels in the brain-mind that can bring us to that place I call home base.

Working with executives in high-pressured jobs, I experienced firsthand the far-reaching effects of negative stress in our society. Teaching professional people to reduce their stress through mind training and meditation can have a huge impact on effectiveness in the workplace. A great example is the research done with airline pilots who had recently been trained to fly the new large transport planes. Within a short period of time, many of the pilots began to burn out, but a few were able to adapt and continue their flight schedule. What the researchers found was that the latter pilots had, while flying, periodically shifted from beta's narrow conceptual focus into a more diffused alpha state of mind. They used their mind to shift into the awareness of the moment. It reduced their stress and thus the wear and tear on their bodies.

As you awaken to a new state of awareness through mind train-ing, you may begin to realize that a fast-paced life does not feel much like home for you. From what we've explored about the brain, mind, and meditation, you know that there is a refuge inside you with a brain-mind that is ready to open into an entirely different space. From the exercises and practices, you know how to shift out of reactive thinking into other levels of the mind, or how to cultivate other levels of consciousness. In this process of waking up to your true self, you will fall in and out of an awakened state and go back to sleepwalking. But you now have some tools to move back into the full awareness of the present moment once again. In that moment, you can once again respond to the gestalt of all things present.

What we have found in our exploration of the brain's neuro-plasticity is that we are in a continual state of evolution that is being consciously propelled by our minds. When you are present in the moment, there is shift in the six-layered cellular structure of the brain's neocortex. The brain's functioning is highly important in reducing stress, which allows conscious awareness to increase. In the nervous system, awareness is increased when large neural patterns fire in tandem in physically distinct regions, connecting neurons throughout the body and routing them through the cortex's six layers of brain cells.

If you recall from part I, the top three layers monitor the automatic thoughts of planning, memory, and decision-making. As the neural networks fire in tandem, the top three layers of cells are dissolved by the lower three layers, which regulate our direct-focused experiences. When the lower three layers of cellular components are synchronous, the alpha, theta, and delta brain waves are activated and there is a cellular cortical shift.

The amazing thing about this process is that it all happens in just six layers of cells in the brain's cortex before we become aware of any content. As the neural activities simultaneously fire off all the brain waves, the prefrontal lobe is reshaped in response to this brain stimulation. Thus, the reshaping of the brain directly strengthens the self-regulation mechanism between the cortex and the limbic system, and therefore directly reduces emotional reactions and stress. This synchrony of neuronal connections stimulates the mind so that it becomes integrated and dispels the automatic negative thoughts of fear and anxiety; this creates receptivity to bliss, happiness, and peace. The cellular dissolve of automatic emotional reactions occurs as you are in "presence."

Presence simply means that you experience things as they are actually occurring and not as your projections from conditioned beliefs, perceptions, and attitudes. You are no longer the prisoner of your mind enslaved to negative, intense emotional reactions. The present moment stops the enslavement of responses. You hold the key to unlock the prison of your mind. The real glory of meditation lies not in any method but in the continual experience of an expanding sense of presence.

When life calls for your mind to have a narrow focus, it is there for your use. Being able to move easily between broad and narrow bands of awareness means you are becoming free and flexible. You will not lose your various emotional responses. You can be happy but also sad; you can be empty but also full; you may not know where you are going but also know how to get there—wherever "there" is. All these various responses are signs that you are not entrapped, and when you live in that wisdom, you are home free.

Bibliography

Part I

Begley, Sharon. "How the brain rewires itself." *Time* 169 (2007): 72–79.

_____. "How thinking can change the brain." *Wall Street Journal* (January 19, 2007).

_____. *Train Your Mind, Change Your Brain.* New York: Ballantine, 2007.

Bremner, Douglas, J. *Does Stress Damage the Brain?* New York: W. W. Norton, 2005.

Brink, Susan. "Study: Romantic love affects brain like drug addiction." *Los Angeles Times* (September 4, 2007).

Dahlberg, Carrie Peyton. "Red brains vs blue brains." *Sacramento Bee* (September 10, 2007).

Damasio, Antonio. *The Feeling of What Happens.* San Diego, CA: Harcourt Brace, 1999.

Davidson, Richard J., Jon Kabat-Zinn, Jessica Schumacher, et al. "Alterations in brain and immune function produced by mindfulness meditation." *Psychosomatic Medicine* 65 (2003): 564–570.

Dispenza, Joe. *Evolve Your Brain.* Deerfield Beach, FL: Health Communications, 2007.

Doidge, Norman. *The Brain That Changes Itself.* New York: Viking, 2007.

Economist editorial staff. "Who do you think you are? A survey of the brain." *Economist* 381(2006):78–79.

Fulton, F. J., and C. F. Jacobsen. [The functions of the frontal lobes: A comparative study in monkeys and chimpanzees and man.] *Advances in Modern Man* (Moscow) 4 (1935): 113–123.

Gallese, V., L. Fadiga, L. Fogassi, and G. Rizzolatti. "Action recognition in the premotor cortex." *Brain* 119 (1996): 593–609.

Goldberg, Elkhonon. *The Executive Brain.* New York: Oxford University Press, 2001.

Goleman, Daniel. *Destructive Emotions.* New York: Bantam, 2003.

Grubin, David (producer). *The Secret Life of the Brain.* PBS documentary, 2002.

Howard, Pierce J. *The Owner's Manual for the Brain.* Austin: Bard Press, 2006.

Lazar, S. W., C. Kerr, R. H. Wasserman, et al. "Meditation experience is associated with increased cortical thickness. *NeuroReport* 16 (2005): 1893–1897.

Linden, David J. *The Accidental Mind.* Cambridge, MA: Belknap Press of Harvard University Press, 2007.

Lipton, Bruce H. *The Biology of Belief.* Santa Rosa, CA: Mountain of Love/ Elite Books, 2005.

Lutz, Antoine, Lawrence L. Greischar, Nancy B. Rawlings, et al. "Long-term meditators self-induce high-amplitude gamma synchrony during mental practice." *Proceedings of the National Academy of Sciences of the USA* 101 (2004): 16369–16373.

Lykken, David T., and Auke Tellegen. "Happiness is a stochastic phenomenon." *Newsweek* 128 (1996): 52–59.

Newberg, Andrew, and Mark Robert Waldman. *How God Changes Your Brain: Breakthrough Findings from a Leading Neuroscientist.* New York, Ballantine, 2009.

Pearce, Joseph Chilton. *The Biology of Transcendence.* Rochester, VT: Park Street Press, 2002.

Rakic, P. "Neurogenesis in adult primate neocortex: An evaluation of the evidence." *Nature Reviews Neuroscience* 3 (2002) :65–71.

Ricard, Matthieu. *Happiness.* New York: Little, Brown, 2006.

Rosenzweig, M. R., and E. L. Bennett. "Psychobiology of plasticity: Effects of training and experience on brain and behavior." *Behavioral Brain Research* 78 (1996): 57–65.

Sapolsky, Robert M. *Why Zebras Don't Get Ulcers.* New York: Times Books, 2004.

Segal, Zindel V., J. Mark G. Williams, and John D. Teasdale. *Mindfulness-Based Cognitive Therapy for Depression.* New York: Guilford Press, 2002.

Siegel, Daniel J. *The Mindful Brain.* New York: W. W. Norton, 2007.

Siegel, Daniel J., and Mary Hartzell. *Parenting from the Inside Out.* New York: J. P. Tarcher/Putnam, 2004.

Soutar, Richard. Doing *Neurofeedback*, Self-published by Richard Soutar, 2002.

Sternberg, Esther, M. *The Balance Within*. New York: W. H. Freeman, 2000.

Thakore, J. H., and T. G. Dinan. "Growth hormone secretion: The role of glucocorticoids." *Life Sciences* 55 (1994): 1083–1099.

Wallace, B. Alan, and Brian Hodel. *Embracing Mind*. Boston: Shambhala, 2008.

Part II

Almaas, A. H. *Facets of Unity: The Enneagram of Holy Ideas*. Berkeley, CA: Diamond Books, 1998.

Austin, James H. *Zen-Brain Reflections*. Cambridge, MA: MIT Press, 2006.

Baron, Renee, and Elizabeth Wagele. *The Enneagram Made Easy*. San Francisco, CA: HarperSanFrancisco, 1994.

Braverman, Eric R. *The Edge Effect*. New York: Sterling, 2004.

_____. Younger You. New York: McGraw Hill, 2007.

Brizendine, Louann. *The Female Brain*. New York: Morgan Road Books. 2006.

Cade, C. Maxwell, and Nona Coxhead. *The Awakened Mind*. New York: Delacorte Press/Eleanor Friede, 1979.

Cahn, B. R., and J. Polich. "Meditation states and traits: EEG, ERP, and neuroimaging studies." *Psychological Bulletin* 132 (2006): 180–211.

Daniels, David N., and Virginia A. Price. *The Essential Enneagram*. San Francisco, CA: HarperSanFrancisco, 2000.

Fehmi, Les, and Jim Robbins. *Open Focus*, Boston: Trumpeter, 2007.

Howe-Murphy, Roxanne. *Deep Coaching*. Ennneagram Press (lifewise coaching.com), 2007.

Jaxon-Bear, Eli. *From Fixation to Freedom: The Enneagram of Liberation*. Ashland, OR: Leela Foundation Press, 2001.

Kabat-Zinn, Jon. *Coming to Our Senses*. New York: Hyperion Press, 2003.

_____. *Full Catastrophe Living*. New York: Delacorte Press, 1990.

Kaufman, Marc. "Meditation gives brain a charge, study finds." *Washington Post* (January 3, 2005).

Lieberman, Matthew D., Naomi L. Eisenberger, Molly J. Crockett, et al. "Putting feelings into words: Affect labeling disrupts amygdala activity in response to affective stimuli." *Psychological Science* 18 (2007): 421–428.

Linden, David J. *The Accidental Mind*. Cambridge, MA: Belknap Press of Harvard University Press, 2007.

251

Lowan, John, and Paul Petty. *NeuroWave: The Art and Science of Meditation.* Victoria, BC: Peak Life Technologies, 2005.

Maitri, Sandra. *The Spiritual Dimension of the Enneagram.* New York: Jeremy P. Tarcher/Putnam, 2000.

Menon, Devdas. *Stop Sleep Walking Through Life!* Mumbai, India: Yogi Impressions, 2004.

Nishijima, Gudo Wafu. "The relation between the autonomic nervous system and Buddhism." Conference paper, Brussels, 2002.

Palmer, Helen. *The Enneagram in Love and Work.* San Francisco, CA: HarperSanFrancisco, 1995.

Raz, A. and J. Buhle. "Typologies of attentional networks." *Nature Reviews Neuroscience* 7 (2006): 367–379.

Rinpoche, Sogyal. *Glimpse after Glimpse.* San Francisco, CA: HarperSanFrancisco, 1995.

Riso, Don Richard, and Russ Hudson. *Personality Types: Using the Enneagram for Self- Discovery.* Boston: Houghton Mifflin, 1996.

_____. *Understanding the Enneagram.* Boston, Houghton Mifflin, 2000.

_____. *The Wisdom of the Enneagram,* New York: Bantam, 1999.

Robbins, Jim. *A Symphony in the Brain.* New York: Atlantic Monthly Press, 2000.

Salzberg, Sharon, and Joseph Goldstein. *Insight Meditation.* Louisville, CO: Sounds True, 2001.

Shapiro, Francine. *Eye Movement Desensitization and Reprocessing (EMDR).* New York: Guilford Press, 2001.

Taylor, Jill Bolte. *My Stroke of Insight.* New York: Viking, 2006.

Wallace, B. Alan. *The Attention Revolution.* Boston: Wisdom Publications, 2006.

Wise, Anna. *Awakening the Mind.* New York: Jeremy P. Tarcher/Putnam, 2002.

_____. *The High-Performance Mind.* New York: Putnam, 1995.

Appendix: Meditation CDs

For maximum benefit from the brain-wave meditations, I encourage you to use my meditation CDs or mp3 downloads of the meditations. The CDs are a significant way to train your mind. I find it impossible to read the meditations and allow the mind to go into deeper meditative states. Reading the meditations will keep your mind in beta, reducing the deep relaxation that is needed. There are binaural frequency pulsations in the background on each CD that not only increase the effectiveness of the meditations, but also much more rapidly increase your mental and emotional stability and the rewiring of your brain. On my website (www.healrewireyourbrain.com), you will find the binaural meditations under "Heal Your Mind, Rewire Your Brain Meditations." You can also obtain CDs of the meditations from Amazon or download the mp3s from iTunes.

In the background of each meditation CD or mp3 download, there is the binaural beat that corresponds to the particular brain wave of that meditation. It is the brain's response in listening to two slightly different frequencies that alters the brain wave. Each brain wave has its own binaural beat that reinforces each brain wave and enables the listener to experience the meditation more deeply as I guide you through it. Research reports changes in consciousness associated with binaural beats. Listening to binaural beats may be relaxing or stimulating, depending on the frequency of the binaural beat.

Binaural beats in the beta frequency have been associated with increased concentration or alertness, vividness, and clarity. Binaural beats in the alpha frequency have been associated with increased alpha brain waves in memory. Binaural beats in the theta and delta ranges have been associated with deepened, relaxed creativity and deep meditative states.

Over time, with the aid of the binaural beats, you will find that your brain comes into synchrony more easily, as the beats support the rewiring of your brain for peace, health, and well-being.

The use of binaural beats began with Heinrich Wilhelm Dove. a Prussian physicist and meteorologist who, in 1839, discovered that the brain produced an altered state in brain waves when presented with two slightly different frequencies (sounds) played separately to each ear. When signals of two different frequencies are heard, one in each ear, the brain detects phase differences between these signals. The brain processes the information of these waves differently and integrates the two signals, producing the sensation of a third "beat." The brain response is a binaural beat from two slightly different frequencies with fluctuating rhythm of the difference between the two auditory inputs. The difference between the two frequencies must be small (below about 30 Hz) for the effect to occur; otherwise, the two tones will be heard separately and no beat will be perceived. The benefit of the third beat enhances your ability to move into each brain wave meditation more easily and deeply. The addition of the binaural beat helps you relax your body; reduce thoughts, anxiety, and stress; and focus and concentrate in each brain-wave meditation. These binaural beats and the mental tools of intention, attention, receptivity, and awareness promote brain synchrony and thus the rewiring of the brain. Today, we use headphones or speakers to produce this effect.

Here are the meditations covered in this book that are available on CD or as a download to make it easier for you to do the meditations and reap the benefits:

Beta Relaxation Meditation

Alpha Perception Meditation #1

Alpha Perception Meditation #2

Theta Wisdom Meditation #1

Theta Wisdom Meditation #2

Delta Synchrony Meditation

Index